PARTICIPATION PROGRAMS IN WORK ORGANIZATIONS

PARTICIPATION PROGRAMS IN WORK ORGANIZATIONS

Past, Present, and Scenarios for the Future

AVIAD BAR-HAIM

QUORUM BOOKS
Westport, Connecticut • London

Library of Congress Cataloging-in-Publication Data

Bar-Haim, Aviad.
    Participation programs in work organizations : past, present, and scenarios for the
future /Aviad Bar-Haim.
        p. cm.
    Includes bibliographical references and index.
    ISBN 1–56720–423–6 (alk. paper)
    1. Management—Employee participation. I. Title.
HD5650.B164 2002
331'.01'12—dc21   2001051095

British Library Cataloguing in Publication Data is available.

Library of Congress Catalog Card Number: 2001051095
ISBN: 1–56720–423–6

First published in 2002

Quorum Books, 88 Post Road West, Westport, CT 06881
An imprint of Greenwood Publishing Group, Inc.
www.quorumbooks.com

Printed in the United States of America

The paper used in this book complies with the
Permanent Paper Standard issued by the National
Information Standards Organization (Z39.48–1984).

10 9 8 7 6 5 4 3 2 1

for Rachi

Contents

Part IV: Future of Participation Programs

Acknowledgments

I am grateful to the following persons for their valuable comments. Responsibility for the opinions and errors lies with the author alone:

Prof. Rivka Bar-Yosef—Department of Sociology and Anthropology, the Hebrew University in Jerusalem, Israel.
Prof. Ruth Ben-Israel—Buchmann Faculty of Law, Tel-Aviv University, Israel.
Prof. Amira Galin—Faculty of Management, Tel-Aviv University, Israel.
Dr. Giora Kulka—History Department, Open University of Israel.
Prof. Hans-Erich Mueller—FHW-Berlin School of Economics.
Prof. Derek S. Pugh—The Open Business School at the Open University, UK.
Prof. Menachem Rosner—The Institute for the Research of the Kibbutz and the Cooperative Idea, Haifa University, Israel.

Also, I wish to thank my publisher, Mr. Eric Valentine and his colleagues in Quorum Books for their encouragement, patience and professionalism.

Permission to use citations is gratefully acknowledged:

- AK Press Distribution, 674-A 23rd Street, Oakland, CA 94612 USA www.akpress.org: Excerpts from "The Challenge of Mondragon" by George Benello, in *Reinventing Anarchy Again,* edited by Howard Ehrlich (AK Press, 1996).
- Walter de Gruyter GmbH & Co. KG Genthiner Strasse 13 D-10785 Berlin/ Germany: *Excerpts from Models of Industrial Democracy: Consultation, Co-determination and Workers' Management* by Charles D. King and Mark van de Vall. 1978 (ISBN: 90 279 7834 6).

Introduction

This book is about employees' participation programs in work organizations. The theme is an old one in the social sciences, and its multidimensional and enigmatic character both attracts and frustrates researchers. Similar to some other fuzzy concepts in the social sciences, it lacks ontological and epistemological consensus on its definition, measurement, and application. This is evident in recurrent debates among researchers on the assessment and interpretation of research findings in the field. Despite extensive research in field, participation in work organizations still has ill-defined status as a subject of rigorous academic inquiry. This should not surprise any student of participation. Its interdisciplinary character; its ideological, political, and managerial biases; its being a subject of uneasy discourse among scientists and practitioners; its cultural diversity; its different historical contexts—all these distinctive factors hinder attempts at integration.

Yet, is integration needed? The correct answer is Yes and No.

Yes, because integrative and coherent sets of concepts, tools, and theories enable us to focus on specific problem areas and enhance the accumulation of valid, reliable, and useful information within the research community. To paraphrase Kuhn's terminology, it also better exhausts the knowledge paradigm, and the body knowledge is thus more systematic and comprehensive.

No, because the cost of integrating a diversified and immature field might be too high in terms of oversimplification and reductionism. Also, ignoring too many specific aspects and unique cases may undermine the application utility of the field, and consequently violate the famous dictum of Kurt Lewin—that nothing is more useful than a good theory. So, the attempt of integration in the case of participation is perhaps noble, but is not necessarily worthwhile and there are risks.

However, the four parts of this book are an attempt to navigate this intellectual stormy ocean. Part I surveys the intellectual and pragmatic roots of participation programs in work organizations and maps the main forms and practices of these programs. Part II, a historical dimension, divides the period after World War II into "two generations": The first generation is the first three decades after the war, in which the dominant and popular programs in many countries were of the "indirect workers' participation" type. The second generation belongs to the last decades, and is characterized by the "direct participation" type. The analytical tool in this part is a presentation of "major players" in each generation, as strong examples.

An attempt is made in Part III to construct a general model to explain the emergence, development (or degeneration), and performance of any participation program in work organizations. In the framework of this model, participation programs are perceived as open systems, which first, have to survive and second, have to contribute useful products to their context environment. Five components are identified as indispensable and necessary to any participation program, albeit with many possible options and configurations. These components are goals, support, participants, participatory practices, and contributions. The five components constitute a core program, which is practiced in four context areas: strategy, individual, organizational, and performance. With a small set of variables, the model enables us to better understand the rich world of participation programs that is described in the book. Nevertheless, two case studies are presented in detail as examples of the model's potential and as an invitation to further elaboration and refinement of studies of participation.

The conclusion in Part IV attempts to look at the future of participation programs as an organizational and social phenomenon.

Part I

Participation Programs: Mapping the Field

Workers' or employee participation belongs to a family of themes, including industrial democracy, employee involvement, autonomous work group, and self-management. Each of these ideas is complicated and has a unique history. Different people define each theme in a different way. This may explain the convergence, in which academic discussions have been mingled with political propaganda, labor and management philosophies, and practical programs of participation. However, the common ground of all this intellectual and organizational thinking and experience is a realization that there are basic human and organizational problems that need solutions in the world of work.

There is another related family that I shall *not* discuss in this book, and that is participation as a desired way of life, as an end worthy for its own sake in all spheres of life—in work, in consumption, in education, in culture, and in every aspect of social life. The variety of organizational forms that have been built on this ideal is spread from "weak" forms of productive and consumptive cooperatives to "strong" forms like the Israeli kibbutz and other communes. The ideal of the participatory commune is not a "solution" to the industrial civilization, to use Elton Mayo's term. It is an alternative. However, the reader may get a flavor of this alternative from the Mondragon case in Appendix C.

Chapter 1

Problem Areas and Definitions

There are three problem areas at the workplace level that require participatory solutions:

1. Industrial democracy and power sharing at the workplace level
2. Reduction of work alienation[1]
3. Effective human resource management

INDUSTRIAL DEMOCRACY

The problem with democracy at the workplace stems from a lack of equality of rights and political opportunities for employees. This inequality is in contrast with the formal equality in the world outside the workplace—the civil society. Not surprisingly, industrial democracy and workers' participation are ideas that were developed during the Industrial Revolution and the emergence of the democratic nation state. The year 1830 is a landmark in the Industrial Revolution: "What is certain is that by 1830 Britain had, in one way or another, obtained a body of wage-paid workers, acclimatized to factory conditions and able to move from place to place, and from employment to employment" (Ashton, 1948, 125–126).

What seemed to Ashton as acclimatization, namely, adaptation and acceptance of the existing reality by people who lacked other ways to make a living, was evaluated by Crossland as the origin of the ideas about industrial democracy and workers' participation: "Historically, the aspiration towards a 'justier' organization of industry has been enshrined in the demand for industrial democracy or workers' control.

This has a long history in the Labour Movement, stretching back to Owen's ambitious Operative Builders' Union . . ." (Crossland, 1963, 257).

The aspiration for a just industry was followed by a challenge against the ideology of the new industrial order and the changes in the social status of workers. The essence of these changes was the disengagement of the new employers from the older social and moral responsibilities to the lower classes, now comprising most of the new industrial work-force. New ideologies or new myths justified this disengagement: "The Industrial Revolution and the breakdown of the traditional way of life were justified by the religious ethics (the Protestant ethics) . . . and the scientific explanations for the achievement of economic success (the Social Darwinism)" (Herzberg, 1966, 33–34).

However, the workers in this system refused to play the assigned role (Herzberg, 1966): "But, as time passed, the workers could not tolerate a system in which most of them were defined as unfit and damned and their ill treatment by management so justified." The workers had another strong reason to resist the new managerial ideologies. These ideologies were incompatible with the no less effective ideals of the time—those of democracy. Thus, the class struggle was fueled not only by the conflict in the production relations but also by the conflict between the production relations and the ideal of democracy: "The revolutionary threat to an emerging industrial society involves the workers' quest for civic recognition in that society; it involves a struggle between classes over rights of which the workers claim to have been deprived unjustly and which they seek to regain through a political struggle for a more equitable distribution within industrial society" (Bendix, 1956, 437). And Cole elaborates on this intolerable deprivation: "No society can rest on a really democratic basis unless it applies the democratic method to its industrial as well as to its political affairs . . ." (Cole, 1957, 10).

Nominal participation in decisions that determine personal and collective fate is a basic individual right in a modern society, although professional officials and public representatives run state affairs. Cole clarifies this delicate contradiction (Cole, 1957, 12): "No one expects the ordinary voter to be equipped with the knowledge and capacity needed for drafting a parliamentary bill, or even local government project. What he is required to do as a participant in political action is to vote . . . and to make his voice heard."

Sartory (1965) and other political scientists, like Dahl and Schumpeter believed that modern democracies ought to be indirect and governed by delegates, because history shows that democracies based on direct participation turned out to be very fragile. However, Pateman (1970, I, II), who made a most insightful analysis on workers' participation and industrial democracy, suggested that representative democracy cannot replace participatory democracy, namely, direct participation of all employees in their workplace. Observing that representative democracy in industry exists normally only through trade unions outside the workplace itself, one cannot ignore the insufficiency of this solution to the problem of industrial democracy. Strauss and Rosenstein revealed this irony even in socialist circles: "Socialist writers of the reformist school, such as the British Fabians and the German revisionists, rejected the idea of workers' control at the workplace level as being incompatible with efficiency . . . Behind this rejection of direct workers' control was a mistrust of workers' abilities to prefer the interests of the public to their own narrow ones" (Strauss and Rosenstein, 1970, 201).

This statement is not accurate regarding three famous Fabians: the Webbs and G. D. H. Cole. Democratization of the workplace is central to Cole's theory. He rejects the Marxist solution on the one hand and the Anarchist solution on the other hand: "What . . . is the fundamental evil in our modern society which we should set out to abolish?" (Cole, 1975, 62). Cole assured us that many intelligent people would answer wrongly (Cole, 1975, 65–66): "They would answer poverty, when they ought to answer slavery . . . Poverty is the symptom: slavery the disease . . . ."

This is a political approach par excellence. Poverty is a superstructure in power relations, and as it is well known, an important part of Cole's solution is workers' control in the workplace (in collaboration with the employers, the consumers, and the government). Cole relied on the work of Sidney and Beatrice Webb. Fritz Naftali (1944, 163) told us that the term *industrial democracy* first entered the Labour Movement's vocabulary via the Webbs's book with the same title. In their book the Webbs claimed that trade unions in modern industrial systems are exemplary democratic organizations (Webb, 1902, 847): "In the Anglo-Saxon world of today [1897], we find that Trade Unions are democracies: that is to say, their internal constitutions are all based on the principles of 'government of the people, by the people, for the people' . . . ."

They believed that a democratic regime in industry is possible if an economic, social, and political equilibrium is attained among consumers, producers, workers, and the government (Webb, 821–822):

"Thus, it is for the consumers . . . to decide what shall be produced. It is for the directors of industry to decide how it shall be produced . . . and it is for the expert negotiators of the Trade Unions . . . to state the terms under which each grade will sell its labor . . . To its (the community) elected representative and trained civic service is entrusted the duty of . . . considering the permanent interests of the State as a whole."

Thus, I believe that the Fabians were the first to suggest a comprehensive democratization program in industry. Although Guild Socialism and workers' control according to Cole's program were never attained anywhere, Blumberg (1968, 193–195) suggested that the self-management system of Yugoslavia before that country's disintegration was inspired by the Fabian thinking.

Nevertheless, industrial democracy and workers' participation have become relevant only after World War II, and not before the disillusionment of other measures of democratization in industry, namely, recognition of labor unions and/or nationalization of major industries in many countries (Blumberg, 1968, 2). Apparently, these policies have not changed the basic lack of democracy beyond the gates of work organizations. In some countries the cost of labor union recognition in "democracy currency" was detrimental. In the United States, the cost of recognition in labor unions, as expressed in Wagner Law (1935), was prohibitive to the institution of industrial democracy on the workplace level. This was the conclusion of a symposium held by the Woodrow Wilson Center for International Scholars, which has been summarized and edited by Lichtenstein and Harris (1993). Thus, for example, David Montgomery showed there (Lichtenstein and Harris, Chap. 2) how the term industrial democracy was first used by trade unionists to describe their conception of the workplace based on social and political democratic principles. But the National Association of Manufacturers made this term synonymous with the "open shop" policy that was aimed at undermining the unions' power.

Thus, oligarchy and bureaucratic rule have continued to control the workplace—private or public, unionized or not—and the demand for industrial democracy and workers' participation has not vanished.

WORK ALIENATION

Workers' alienation inspires many programs of workers' participation, because the programs are based on the hope that alienation can be reduced, if not eliminated, through participation. Marx was the first to discuss work alienation comprehensively. Unlike many philosophers and social thinkers of his time, he identified the alienation as a psychological problem and not as a political one. Political privileges as part of power are superstructures above the production relations, not vice versa. The class struggle is over control of the means of production. However, at the individual worker's level, the problem is a lack of meaningful life, a lack of opportunities to be a full creative person (Homo Faber).As a human being, a worker aspires to self-expression via processing his or her physical and intellectual environment. However, this aspiration is abandoned in the mass production relations and therefore is doomed to alienation, and in Marx's words:

In what does . . . alienation of labor consist? First, that the work is external to the worker, that is not part of his nature, that consequently he does not fulfill himself, has a feeling of misery, not of well-being, does not develop freely a physical and mental energy, but is physically exhausted and mentally debased. The worker, therefore, feels himself at home only during his leisure, whereas at work he feels homeless. His work is not voluntary but imposed, forced labour. It is not the satisfaction of a need, but only a means for satisfying another need. Finally, the alienated character of work for the worker appears in the fact that it is not his work but work for someone else, that in work he does not belong to himself but to another person (Coser and Rosenberg, 1976, 378).

So, for Marx there are four objects of alienation: the *product,* which is produced by the worker; the *process* of which the worker is a part; the worker's *personality*; and the workplace's *social environment.* Marx elaborated largely on the first three objects, which reflect two major facets of alienation: meaninglessness of work and powerlessness of the worker in the prevailing production relations. The worker has no control over the kind, quantity, and quality of the product that he or she produces. These are dictated by the capitalist and managerial system and by the mass production technology. In this system workers are forced to ignore their most basic personal needs, and to fit themselves into an alien coercive system (Schacht, 1970, 115–119).

Workers' social disengagement and loneliness, which are expressed in the social alienative character of the workplace, are mainly negative side effects, which need their separate treatment, but are not the social disease itself. Marx did not ignore the social needs of the worker. However, this category in his alienation theory remained underdeveloped, and only later works in the field have elaborated this dimension (Schacht, 1970, 168–173).

Many students of alienation have adopted the anthropological image of the Homo Faber as a departure point. However, they explored social belonging and identification as additional dimensions of alienation. The lack of these elements is thought to be just as serious as powerlessness and meaninglessness, to take two of the five major types of alienation that have been formulated by Seeman (1959). Accordingly, the human problem of the worker is not merely the inability to be creative in his or her work, but also the lack of supportive and challenging social framework. Blauner (1964), who examined empirically the alienation typology of Seeman, explicates these added elements (Blauner, 1964, 6): "Alienation exists when workers are unable to control their immediate work processes, to develop a sense of purpose and function which connects their jobs to overall organization of production, to belong to integrated industrial communities, and when they fail to become involved in the activity of work as a mode of personal self-expression."

In a series of four case studies of work under different technologies, Blauner made a strong case for the importance of technology among determinants of work alienation. However, in his particular analysis of textile work, in one of the four cases he did not find as high a level of alienation as his theory had projected, and the technology factor proved inadequate. He argued that many textile workers worked only for wages, without an intrinsic orientation to work. Therefore, they did not find the objective, alienating conditions of their work as hard to take. Moreover, many textile workers derived their life's real meaning through the closely connected mill communities, their families, and their traditional way of life. These social bonds mitigated the dissatisfying work and the expected work alienation. Blauner concluded that for the textile workers the more pervasive dimensions were isolation and self-estrangement. In reassessing Blauner's study in the textile industry (based on 1947 data), Leiter (1985) replicated most of Blauner's findings, but his explanations for less alienation among "traditional" workers (women, Southerners, etc.) were unsupported.

The multifaceted approach of Seeman and Blauner is not typical of the alienation literature, in which there is a split between the psychological and the sociological approach. Both Schacht (1970, 161–164) and Israel (1971) noticed in their profound analyses, that a contradiction exists between the concept of alienation in the writings of psychologists like Fromm (1955) or Riesman (1961) and those of sociologists like Durkheim, Mayo, Parsons, and Merton. From a psychological point of view, a major symptom of alienation is conformity in the modern mass society. Conformity is a danger to a person's uniqueness and creativity, and, thus a danger to his or her well-being. For Durkheim and Mayo, conformity was a desired state. They worried more about the social well-being. Therefore, they saw a danger in the absence of strong centers for social conformity and identification. They were concerned about anomic disintegration of social institutions in the era of industrialization, specialization, and bureaucratization (Mayo, 1945, Chap. 1). From a different point of view, Parsons aimed at the same concept when he defined alienation as the inability to integrate in the social structure and to internalize societal values and norms. His definition of alienation (1951, 233) is "A possible product of something going wrong in the process of value acquisition through identification."

Felix Geyer and Walter Heinz (1992), in an assessment of the state of alienation research, defined alienation as an umbrella concept, uniting loosely related dimensions. Accordingly, Marxists, who tended to consider alienation as an objective state, criticized Seeman for concentrating too much on subjective states of individuals, such as their feelings of powerlessness, and neglecting their reality and the social structures that cause these feelings. Anyway, research showed convergence of the various approaches and attempts at discovering strategies for de-alienation, such as participation and self-management. Eventually, the differences between the psychological approach and the sociological approach became, perhaps, blurred. The apparent contradictions may result from a different level of analysis of the same phenomenon. For example, workers' participation may be used as a cure to the alienation disease, which has both psychological and sociological pathologies.

An integrative approach of this sort was proposed in the human motivation theory of Abraham Maslow (1943). He identified five groups of human needs: physical existence, security, belonging, social recognition, and self-actualization. He hypothesized that these groups of needs are arranged in a hierarchy, in such a way that there are lower needs and higher needs. The higher needs are addressed only when the lower ones are satisfied. Thus, humans are motivated to satisfy their basic physical and security needs. Only then arise the relatedness needs (belonging and social recognition), and, finally, when all other needs are met, the self-actualization needs become operative.

The original notion of Maslow's hierarchy of human needs was not substantiated empirically.[2] However, it offered an interesting solution to the multiple facets of work alienation. Westley (1972) used this model in analyzing workers' participation programs. He suggested that in poor countries, which employ poorly educated and unskilled workers, the workforce interest in participation programs would be low, because workers struggle for survival, and will not be attracted by programs that offer mainly social and psychological rewards. On the other hand, workers in richer countries, where they are more educated and established, may respond more favorably to social and psychological benefits of these programs.

Blumberg suggested a different solution, a sociological one and basically positivist. He defined alienation as a state of dissatisfaction in work on several dimensions, partly objective (absenteeism, turnover, industrial relations conflicts, etc.), and partly subjective (job attitudes, morale, etc.). In an in-depth survey of three decades of research he summarized (Blumberg, 123): "There is hardly a study in the entire literature which fails to demonstrate that satisfaction in work is enhanced or that other generally acknowledged beneficial consequences accrue from genuine increase in workers' decision-making power . . . ."

Thus, Blumberg generalized states of alienation to feelings of dissatisfaction, and then cited rich evidence to support the idea that work dissatisfaction can be reduced by workers' participation. He also suggested that reducing alienation by increasing workers' power in decision making is more effective in reducing alienation than other solutions, such as automation, job redesign, and nonwork alternatives (Blumberg, Chap. 4).[3] Support for Blumberg's argument was found in numerous studies. Argyris (1973), for example, cited findings from the industrial clinical psychology, which pointed to the limitations of solutions for clinical problems of workers who lack genuine participation in decision-making. Parnell and Bell (1994) brought a newer array of studies that support Blumberg and Argyris.

However, this picture does not tell the whole story. There are studies of that time, which did not support Blumberg's claim; some actually contradicted it. Obradovich (1970), for example, tested Blauner's thesis in Yugoslav industrial enterprises under the regime of self-management, and did not find the expected reduction in feelings of alienation. He proposed the explanation that work is not a central life interest to most workers, and even an extremely participatory program, like the Yugoslav, cannot cure feelings of alienation. Dun (1973) also cited studies that do not support Blumberg's thesis. Yet, the mainstream of the theoretical and practical preoccupation with participation holds the tenet of participation as a cure for work alienation.

EFFECTIVE HUMAN RESOURCE MANAGEMENT

The sociological and psychological literature, and to a certain degree the political science literature as well, is concerned with participation as a solution to problems of equality, freedom, individual self-fulfillment, and the well-being of the working community. However, the organizational and managerial literature is more skeptical and critical of this solution and is inclined to highlight the constraints and limitations of any participatory solution on the workplace level.

Taking the managerial point of departure, one may start with the employers. In the beginning of the twentieth century, the common assumption among employers and managers was that everyone in the work organization—entrepreneurs, managers, as well as workers—are Homo *economicos,* whose sole interest is profit or wages maximization. Therefore the implied action to be taken was to maximize productivity and efficiency (Wren, 1972, Part II). This was the basic premise of the scientific management movement, led by Frederick W. Taylor and others in the first decades of the twentieth century. They asserted that workers would not be interested in decision-making or other managerial responsibilities, and would be satisfied with appropriate material rewards for their efforts.

This instrumental philosophy was espoused by the antidemocratic view of work organizations of that time. Max Weber and Robert Michels were among the first to discuss the question of compatibility between bureaucracy and democracy.[4] They identified the potential conflict between the efficiency principle of the bureaucratic administration, based on hierarchy, specialism, and technical expertise, and the democratic principle of government, based on equality and freedom. Here is Michels' famous "iron law of oligarchy" (1962, 365): "It is organization which gives birth to the dominion of the elected over the electors, of the mandataries over the mandators, of the delegates over the delegators. Who says organization, says oligarchy."

Weber was less determined in his conclusions. He emphasized the technical mechanism of the bureaucratic regime, and did not see such an a priori incompatibility. At this point we may listen to Mouzelis (1975, 26): "Despite Weber's pessimism as to the long term consequences of bureaucratization and his fears about the decline of democracy and individual freedom, he was cautious enough not to draw definite and dogmatic conclusions as to the future dominance of bureaucracy."

Lipset et al. (1956), Wilensky (1956), Edelstein (1967), and others showed in their studies that the iron law of oligarchy is not absolute, and that there are important exceptions to this "law" in several modes of coexistence between democracy and bureaucracy. However, they concluded that there were still strong tendencies of oligarchy and bureaucracy in modern organizations. This conclusion is a logical result of the Weberian model itself. In this model there is no room for participation and democracy in organizations. Actually, there is no room even for more basic psychological and social needs of individuals and groups, or for their political rights. This is because the organization is no more than a legal-rational tool to achieve goals that are set from the outside. Employees accept these goals in advance, before entering the organization, and they are recruited according to their specific skills and abilities.

The impersonal employment contract resolves in advance and in a rational way all the problems of motivation, coordination, rewards, and conflict of interests. It leaves very narrow space for interpersonal natural friction. But even this space is managed rationally and formally by a disciplinary mechanism. The model assumes that people voluntarily enter these contractual relations, and accept the whole package of rules and organizational duties, statuses, present and future roles, and promotion and rewards.

This conception of the organization as a nonpolitical entity, lacking personal ambitions, posits the question of participation and democracy in organizations as redundant and artificial. A prominent representative of this attitude is the sociologist Talcout Parsons. He described the formal organization as a hierarchic system, with three subsystems to deal with the technical, managerial, and institutional functions. Each subsystem has its own tasks, areas of responsibility, performance and command authorities, and appropriate rewards. Up to this point, this is a Weberian approach par excellence.

However, what Weber formulated as probabilistic tendencies was assumed explicitly by Parsons. For him, employee involvement is needed anyway at all organizational levels, and is achieved normally through the functional division of labor, task requirements of coordination, and the work processes. Note his following description of the relationships between managers and operators in the organization

(Parsons, 1960, Part I, 66–67): "The technical expert, in the nature of the case participates in the technically crucial decision . . .the executive has some kind of 'last word.' But this is a veto power, not a capacity to implement, because the executive is powerless to implement or plan implementation without the competence of the expert . . . ."

Thus, Parsons concluded that even in the bureaucratic organization there are enough degrees of freedom for employees to be involved in decision-making (Parsons, 69): "The institutionalization of the relations must typically take a form where the relative independence of each is protected. Since, however, there is an actual hierarchy, since in some sense the 'higher' authority must be able to have some kind of 'last word,' the problem of protection focuses on the status of the lower elements."

This approach undermines the raison d'être of participation programs, because in these programs the working assumption is that the "relative independence" of the "lower elements" is *not* institutionalized naturally, and the relationships between the managerial level and the executive level remain problematic. The lack of legitimization and institutionalization of employee participation was emphasized by other thinkers in the field. For example, Barnard (1970, 66) recognized the subjective character of coordination and participation, and the preponderance [of willingness to cooperate] by "persons in a modern society always lies on the negative side with reference to any particular existing or potential organization."

Barnard saw in coordination a key process in formal organizations, which is achieved by three necessary and sufficient conditions (Barnard, 65): "(i) there are persons able to communicate with each other, (ii) who are willing to contribute action, (iii) to accomplish a common purpose . . . ." This classical assumption has been supported by many research studies, which put the organization, contrary to the popular view and the theoretical reasoning of Parsons, in a vulnerable position—in fact, at the mercy of its employees. Barnard (1966), Simon (1976), Katz and Kahn (1966), and others defined this vulnerability in terms of readiness of employees to contribute and to coordinate their activities with colleagues and other parts of the organization. Therefore they suggested participatory solutions to efficiency and high performance in organizations, as adaptive complementary devices to the bureaucratic regime.

The reactions, however, to the scientific management and the bureaucratic practices emerged, as is well known from within the world of work and management. The Hawthorne experiments in the United

States in the 1930s, the studies of "The American Soldier" in World War II, the Tavistock experiments in the British coal mines in the 1950s, the sociotechnical projects in Scandinavia in the 1960s, the Human Relations school—all these social and intellectual events changed the thinking about the behavior of people in work organizations. Scrutinizing the writings in this school may portray a shift toward serious exploration of the feasibility of participatory solutions to the problem of human resource management.[5]

CONCEPTS, DEFINITIONS, AND TYPES

Following the classical approach to management, Walker (1974, 9) offered this definition to workers' participation: "Workers' participation in management occurs when those below the top of an enterprise hierarchy take part in the managerial function of the enterprise." In a different way, French, Israel, and Aas (1960, 3) focused on "A process in which two or more parties influence each other in making plans, policies or decisions . . . ." They stressed influence, not any specific managerial function. They also ignored the basic structural different positions of employees and management in the work organizations. However, Pateman (1970, 68), who was very much aware of the hierarchic structure of the production relations, built on this approach: "This definition makes clear that participation must be in something, in this case participation in decision making." Then she developed a scale of three degrees of workers' participation (Pateman, 69–74):

1. *Pseudo-participation.* Mere feelings of workers that they participate in decision-making, while in actuality no substantial changes are made in their roles or in the power structure of the workplace.
2. *Partial-participation.* A real state of workers' participation in decisions. However, their participation is confined to minor issues in their immediate work situation or work group, and no structural changes are made to equalize workers' responsibilities and rewards versus managers.
3. *Full-participation.* A full entry of workers and their delegates to all levels of decision-making at the workplace.

In this famous definition we get a comprehensive view of a range of possible configurations of participation programs: from merely participative style schemes to programs of full workers' participation in management.

Adizes (1972, 17–33) added to the definition matrix the concept of industrial democracy. He differentiated between participation and democracy. The former is entrance to decision-making roles, while the latter is a socio-political structure, which enables equal opportunities to this entrance. Indeed, Tannenbaum and Kahn (1958, 50) preceded him on this point: "Participation is often equated with democratic operation . . . however, democracy and participation refer to distinct phenomena. Democracy and democratic processes refer to a type of control structure, that is, the way in which control is distributed and exercised in an organization. Participation on the other hand refers simply to the formal (and informal) entry of members into organizational roles and the expenditure of individual energies in the playing of these roles."

Pateman had a similar argument about the relationship between workers' participation and industrial democracy. Therefore, she preferred to look at the correlation between workers' participation and industrial democracy as a matter of empirical observation, rather than a predetermined assumption (Tannenbaum and Kahn, 73): "In the industrial context, the term 'participation' and 'democracy' cannot be used interchangeably. They are not synonyms. Not only is it possible for partial participation . . . to take place without a democratization of authority structures, but it is also possible for full participation to be introduced at the lower level within the context of a non democratic authority structure overall."

Some researchers equate participation with personal autonomy, which is defined as the amount of freedom a worker has to carry out the job (Spector, 1986). However, participation is distinct from autonomy in that the former involves joint action among two or more people while the latter is limited to the job incumbent to make his or her own decisions. Therefore, participation has an interpersonal element that is lacking in the concept of autonomy.

Recently, Glew et al. (1995) suggested a revised definition. First, they pointed to the lack of a well-developed and widely accepted definition of participation. They cited Dachler and Wilpert (1978, 1), who concluded that "No clear set of questions, let alone of answers, which begin to define the nature of the participation phenomenon are discernible." Second, they synthesized some of the more commonly used definitions in American studies: *influence sharing* (Mitchell, 1973); *joint decision-making* (Locke and Schweiger, 1979); and *employee involvement in decisions* (Miller and Monge, 1986). Third, they offered their own definition: "A conscious and intended effort by individuals at a higher level in an organization to provide visible extra-role or role-expanding opportunities for individuals or groups at a lower level in the organization to have a greater voice in one or more areas of organizational performance."

This definition encompasses participation efforts in a wide variety of initiatives, which differ with respect to whether participation is forced or voluntary, formal or informal, direct or indirect. Participation may also vary in degree from simple consultation to full authority in decision-making, and in scope from a single project to all aspects of the larger work environment. As a consequence, measures of participation may vary substantially. Some would focus on the general participatory culture in the workplace, while others would prefer to focus on the specific arrangements and practices of participation.

Types of Participation Programs: A Synthesis

There are many ways to sort participation programs, and many researchers have offered their own taxonomy or typology. In the 1970s, when the focus of many programs was on participation in managerial decision-making, it was popular to categorize programs according to the decision issues and the organizational level at which decisions were made. Such a typology is suggested by Guest and Knight (1979, 29) and presented in Table 1.1.[6] As we can see in Table 1.1, participation in policy issues and managerial decisions can be done only through indirect representative schemes, while work issues are the natural objects of direct participation schemes.

In a more recent analysis, Knudsen (8–13) employed a similar approach. However, he added a dimension of participation intensity, and distinguished between decision powers and the importance of participation issues. Thus, on this dimension he defined four issues: welfare, operational, tactical, and strategic issues. He observed that programs with a high priority on the issue dimension has a low priority on the decision powers dimension, and vice versa. In practice, direct participation programs with continuous, regular, and heavy load of time and co-determination responsibilities can operate effectively only on operational issues. On the other hand, participation in strategic issues can be accomplished only in the weaker variety of consultation and representative programs. A revised and simplified version of Knudsen's typology is shown in Table 1.2.

In Table 1.2 we can see that for all practical purposes it is sufficient to stay with two basic types of participation: direct participation in

TABLE 1.1. *A Typology of Participation Programs*

Decision issues

Organizational level	Policy issues	long range management issues	current operative issues
Company level	workers' representatives in boards	collective bargaining	
Workplace level		collective bargaining, works councils	
Department/team level			job enrichment, autonomous work group, QWL

operational issues and indirect participation in welfare *and* strategic issues through consultation or co-determination.

The approach in this book is eclectic. The term "participation" is used for a selection of ingredients of several definitions. For that purpose, the approach of Glew et al. is appropriate. However, one basic structural distinction is made and followed: the distinction between *indirect* participation programs by representatives, focused on participation in decision-making (PDM) and programs of *direct* participation on the job or in the work group (OJGP). These are two basic and immanent strategies of participation in work organizations, and to a certain extent, these are the difference between the first generation of workers' participation programs and the second generation of employee involvement programs. Bolweg (1975, 35) makes a distinction between these two routes:[7] On indirect participation: "Indirect forms of participation include all processes and structures whereby workers' representatives

TABLE 1.2. *A Revised Typology of Knudsen for Participation Programs*

Importance of subject

Employee decision making powers	Operational issues	Welfare, Tactical & Strategic issues
Unilateral employee decision (high intensity)	Direct participation	
Co-decision/co-determination (medium intensity)		Indirect participation
Consultation/information (low intensity)		Indirect participation

influence decision-making generally at higher organizational levels, on the workers' behalf . . . ." And on direct participation: "Direct participation focuses on the individual worker and the immediate work group. Under direct participation the worker himself contributes to and influences managerial decision making or executes himself functions previously carried out by management . . . ."

Typologies and taxonomies are analytical tools to comprehend general patterns in complicated phenomena. The cost of sorting by typologies is the loss of the richness, variability, and surprising facets of the phenomenon under investigation. Therefore, I try to use the distinction between indirect and direct participation programs in a loose way—as a general framework in which a rich variety of subtypes and different types of programs are identified, described, and analyzed. In the third part of the book I suggest a theoretical model of participation programs, which enables this dialectical cohabitation of a simplified world of direct programs versus indirect ones, and the reality of countless forms and processes of participation programs.

NOTES

1. Leana and Florkowski (1992), who used the newer terminology, employee involvement programs, defined the motive of human relations, which derives its raison d'être from the work alienation school.

2. See, for example, Schneider and Alderfer (1973).

3. This is, of course, unacceptable for those who see in direct participation on the job or in autonomous work groups a better solution to the problem of alienation, because it touches upon every worker's job, with or without organizational decision-making.

4. Their units of analysis were wider frameworks, such as the public civil service (Weber) and social movements and political parties (Michels). I refer to the workplace as the unit of analysis. However, I find that the analogy is appropriate.

5. For the present discussion, it may be sufficient to suggest several authorities: Elton Mayo (1945), Douglas McGregor (1960), Fredrick Herzberg (1966), and Rensis Likert (1961).

6. Other well-known typologies are those of King and van de Vall, 1969; Tabb and Goldfarb (Galin), 1970, 19.

7. This resembles the distinctions of Lammers, Rosner, and others (personal communication) between political participation and motivational participation.

Chapter 2

Indirect Representative Programs

Representative patterns of workers' participation include arrangements where workers' representatives are connected to a trade union (through membership in local shop committees or holding formal roles in the union's hierarchy) and patterns where there is no such institutional attachment (Bolweg, 1975, 36). In the latter group we find various arrangements of works council and management board participation. However, it is not uncommon to find works councils, joint labor-management committees (JMC), and boards with union representatives or observers.

WORKS COUNCIL

Works councils are joint agencies of employers and employees that discuss labor-related issues such as working conditions, wages, job security, health, and safety, and so on, within an enterprise. In some cases they may conclude works agreements apart from collective labor contracts. The members of works councils represent both union and nonunion employees in an establishment. In many European countries works councils are mandated by legislation, while they are almost nonexistent in North America. Joint labor-management committees in American firms are fundamentally different from the European works councils, because workers in these participation schemes have no formal power independent of the employer.[1]

In a survey of works councils in Europe over a 45-year period, edited by Rogers and Streeck (1995),[2] we get a picture of the historical evolution of works councils in Europe and their current state and role in the workplace industrial relations. Where the employment relations are determined on industry or national levels between employers and labor unions, works councils appear to have consultative or co-determination rights over personnel matters that are not covered by the centralized collective bargaining agreements.[3] In most countries, works councils do not have the legal authority to call strikes, and while the councils in many countries have close ties to the unions, all union and nonunion employees in the workplace elect them. Nevertheless, works councils in most European countries exist in both union and nonunion workplaces. Many observers maintain that works councils have had a positive impact on the firms and the national productivity. However, Olson (1996) noted that there is no compelling empirical evidence to support this claim.

In some historical perspective, we may reveal the contribution of the works council in a different place. The piled-up evidence about the performance of works councils is convincing that as decision-making organs, they have always been weak, slow, and, in many ways, incompetent, not only in comparison to professional management but also in comparison to shop committees and unions. However, if their latent functions have been to soften labor-management relations, to absorb shocks of industrial conflicts, and to make sense of integrative industrial relation systems, then works councils have performed a very important role both in active and proactive manners. In many cases, works councils enabled industrial peace, smooth production processes, and the introduction of technological and organizational innovations.

THE EUROPEAN WORKS COUNCIL

A major innovation in the development of works councils in Europe has been the European Works Council (EWC). This is a new institution that was established by the European Union in 1994.[4] The law ensures that employees and their representatives are properly informed about and consulted on any major transnational issue that affects them. Any multinational or controlling undertaking with at least 1,000 employees in the countries covered by the EWC directive and with at least 150 employees in each of two or more countries falls under the directive's influence. Only genuine 50/50 joint ventures and companies in bankruptcy escape this provision. As in the national works councils, the law doesn't give rights to labor unions to interfere in the running of the

EWCs. However, when labor unions are present within an organization, unions have a major role in the selection of EWC's employee representatives.[5]

Employers are united in opposition to transnational organs like EWCs. Nevertheless, now that EWCs are a reality, employers' attitudes appear to fall into three groups. First, those companies that are heavily unionized and have a history of antagonistic relationships remain opposed to the EWCs. The second group are those with experience with local works councils (Germany, the Netherlands, and, to a lesser degree, France). For them, the main concern is to avoid damaging the smooth operation of the existing arrangements. The third group is employers who have little experience with local works councils, and they attempt to deal with the EWCs in a positive manner. They believe that properly structured and managed information and consultation processes can make a significant contribution to their international competitiveness (Chesters, 1997).

Can we learn about the future of EWCs from the experience of the traditional works councils? The above accounting suggests that some employers do not feel threatened by the new institution. Perhaps more employers will learn in time, as happened with the works councils, that EWCs provide more opportunities and are less threatening than employers originally thought. Nevertheless, there are important differences between the two institutions. The European level of WCs is a constant source of practical and cultural misunderstanding and friction, which requires a lot more resources of communication and solidarity and strains the local works councils. The EWCs enhance job security and employee involvement in strategic decision-making, as has been shown in the case of Renault Belgium, but the benefits over costs for both employees and management are still yet to be seen.

JOINT LABOR-MANAGEMENT COMMITTEES

Joint labor-management committees (JMCs) offer another participative decision-making scheme. Typically, unions and management engage in cooperative efforts in an attempt to resolve troublesome issues, which commonly include incentive pay plans. Labor-management committees, or joint labor-management committees, are already being used by many organizations in the United States, including General Motors and the Internal Revenue Service (IRS), and have been proven effective in reducing absenteeism, turnover, and employee grievances while increasing efficiency and product quality (Schwartz, 1990–91). The American version of JMC, usually set up by collective bargaining, consists of 8 to 12 members with equal representation from unions and management. GM's experience suggested that joint committees were most effective when matters of contract negotiation are avoided. JMCs provide input and recognition for unions and a way for management to respond to complaints and suggestions (Champagne and Chadwin, 1983). Peterson and Tracy (1992) conducted an assessment of the effectiveness of one such joint labor-management committee in a telecommunications firm. The JMC was established to supervise employee involvement and a quality-of-working-life program. The authors found that the work of this steering committee was quite effective.

It is interesting to compare the works councils with the joint labor-management committees. In many practical matters they are similar in that they are a channel for mutual positive communication between labor and management. They both have a consultative character rather than bargaining or decision-making. They both have local coalitions of workplace elites, and they consistently avoid controversial issues (but not necessarily sensitive issues). On the other hand, in terms of sharing and participation, joint labor-management committees, when run properly, are stronger and have more impact on operative issues, not just policy matters. In fact, they display a unique model of a basically representative and indirect organ that has a say on some performance issues on the shop floor. We shall see these characteristics in one of the Israeli programs in Chapter 8.

MANAGEMENT BOARD PARTICIPATION

Another indirect type of worker participation involves workers and union representation on corporate boards of directors (Stern, 1988). Worker and union representation on corporate boards has a long history in Europe with the beginnings of the German co-determination scheme. In the United States the issue gained public attention only in the 1970s, and became a reality when the president of the United Auto Workers (UAW) was appointed to the board of the Chrysler Corporation in 1980. Worker director schemes were initiated by changes in industrial relations policy and corporate law in some countries, and by some firms that started worker director plans on their own initiative (a well-known study of this type documented such experiments in six British firms [Chell, 1983]). These "private" cases in Europe and Australia are important for the U.S. experience, because the example of worker director plans in the United States also developed independently at the firm level rather than through public policy. Legally mandated representation for workers on corporate boards existed in Germany, Sweden, Denmark, Norway, Austria, Luxembourg, and India and in a modified form in the Netherlands as well.

Worker directors are involved in upper-level policy making on long-range issues such as capital investments, products, and marketing. The ability of worker directors to represent employee interests depends on the manner of selecting representatives, their training, their acceptance by other board members, and their ability to report back to constituents. Nevertheless, worker directors face problems of dual loyalty to their workers and union constituencies on the one hand and the corporation and the need for confidentiality on the other hand. They also experience difficulties in working effectively in an unfamiliar environment of the board meetings. The number of worker representatives relative to other board members is also important in determining how worker directors will act to prevent their always being outvoted.

Evaluating worker director schemes from the management perspective produced positive results: Communication and harnessing labor into an overall organizational perspective increased and decisions that might adversely affect labor were explained and understood. There were few confidentiality problems, and the authority of management was not challenged. Other observers (mainly labor officials and pro-labor intellectuals) counter this positive evaluation. From their point of view, the opportunity to democratize the workplace has not been realized. Far worse, workers co-opted by management neglected their duties toward labor interests, and Ramsay (1980) even called this participation scheme "phantom" participation. However, from a pluralist perspective, worker directors have given labor access to information on corporate finances, marketing, and investments that is useful to labor. The presence of worker representatives on boards also has enhanced more consultation with labor and has forced management to be more cautious in making decisions that have implications for job security.

NOTES

1. I am grateful to Professor Hans-Erich Mueller for his comment (personal communication) that works councils are a part of a corporate governance

("a norm pyramid"), which is more than indirect and direct participation, and also includes individual and collective rights, collective agreements, and labor legislation.

2. An earlier comparative study is of Strumthal (1964).

3. In this respect, works councils' activities match many of the activities that are dealt with by local unions in North America.

4. On September 22, 1996, 15 EU members and 3 EFTA members began to implement the required European law about transnational works councils in more than 1,000 multinationals. EU countries:Austria, Belgium, Denmark, Finland, France, Germany, Greece, Ireland, Italy, Luxembourg, Netherlands, Portugal, Spain, Sweden, and the United Kingdom. EFTA countries: Iceland, Liechtenstein, and Norway. Incidentally, at the end of 1996, the new institution faced the first challenge when the French carmaker Renault was alleged to have ignored consultation requirements in closing a plant in Belgium.

5. According to an anonymous report (*People Management,* March 5, 1998, London), the overwhelming majority of employee representatives elected to European works councils are trade union members. A Trades Union Congress (TUC) study of 81 companies based in Belgium, Spain, Germany, France, Ireland, the Netherlands, and the United Kingdom showed that 374 of the 520 British employee representatives were trade union members. Over half the respondents reported that they were selected in direct elections, 18 percent were chosen by delegates, and 7 percent secured a place through a special election by union members. More than two-thirds of respondents said that their experiences on a works council had given them a better understanding of the company. The TUC said that initial fears that works councils would harm trade unionism have not been realized.

Chapter 3

Direct Participation Programs

There are basically three types of direct participation programs: participation via job redesign, participation via autonomous or self-directed work groups, and participation via general processes of work and organizational reform. These programs are better understood when we compare them with the Taylorite or scientific management approach, especially in its mass production or "Fordist" configuration of jobs and work methods. Indeed, the Fordist mass production model is the reference point for all the direct participation programs. Let us recall the core ideas of the scientific management school:

1. Work should be studied scientifically and decomposed to its most basic and simple tasks. This decomposition is required to achieve specialization, expertise, and control of work behavior.
2. The design of work tasks should be scientifically determined in order to find the best way to achieve optimal efficiency. Once a single efficient way of performing the work has been found, all employees should adapt to the standard technical solution.
3. Employees should be selected according to the required skills of the designed jobs, and employers should be careful not to recruit under- or overqualified persons for the vacant jobs.
4. Employees should be trained meticulously for their job, according to the scientific guidelines of job analysis, and with intensive coaching and control.
5. Employees should be motivated by rewards to perform exactly according to the detailed rules and procedures of the designed work. The rewards

should be proportional to the actual quality and quantity of the per-formed work.

In contrast with the scientific management philosophy, the alternative idea was to reject job decomposition and reassemble, enlarge, and enrich the job instead. Indeed, this was the trend of the job-centered programs from the late fifties on, from job enlargement through job enrichment to job redesign. The participatory nature of the reformed jobs in this paradigm is revealed in the changing division of labor and the role of employees in the workflow. In the reformed jobs, employees take responsibility for planning and executing whole sets of tasks, and the gap between thinkers, decision-makers, and doers is thereby narrowed.

Pioneers of this line of thought were social scientists at the Tavistock Institute of Human Relations, established in London in 1946, where the socio-technical theory was developed. In Chapter 5 on the first generation of participation programs, some classical socio-technical projects are referred to, and although old-style socio-technical projects are rare today, such a project has been reported recently on employee participation in pollution reduction (Ruiz-Quintanilla et al., 1996).

William Pasmore (1995) reviewed a rare collection of the early works from which the socio-technical systems theory and practice have developed. He summarized several key insights of the socio-technical system (STS) theory:

1. The work system should be a set of activities making up a functioning whole, rather than a collection of individual jobs.
2. The work group should be more central than individual jobholders.
3. Internal regulation of the work system is preferable to external regulation by supervisors.
4. The design strategy should be based on a redundancy of functions rather than on a redundancy of parts (multi-skilling rather than single-skilling).
5. The discretionary part of work is as important to the success of the system as the prescribed part.
6. The individual worker should be a complement to the machine rather than an extension of it.
7. The designed work should offer increased variety rather than decreased variety, which means that individual and organizational learning is essential to organizational adaptation to change.

Scandinavian writers (Sorensen, 1985; Gustavsen, 1992; Gustavsen and Engelstad, 1985) pointed to the lack of diffusion of STS. In their view, the socio-technical approach was too strongly dominated by external expert knowledge, such as the social scientists at Tavistock. Socio-technical (ST) projects were over-dependent, and could not become self-propelling, nor did they work out as examples of best practice (de Sitter et al., 1997). However, even as merely a "laboratory" experiment, it is well accepted today that the ST movement is one of the most daring and provocative intellectual forces in the theory and practice of participation programs. Many of the ST ideas have been ahead of their time but have lacked the environmental and technological preconditions to effectively spread and assimilate. Also, the unique characters and leadership of the ST group made them a closed zealot, intellectual caste, which was not easy for organizations and "outsider" practitioners to work with. Surprisingly enough, the last decades of the new technologies—the information revolution, the virtual and global networks of organizations and teams, and the urgent needs for organizational and individual learning—have dramatically revived the socio-technical ideas and practices, albeit in revised, more flexible, and more sophisticated modes.

QUALITY OF WORKING LIFE AND HUMANIZATION OF WORK PROGRAMS

Closely related to STS programs, and sometimes working together and focusing on the immediate work environment, are quality of working life (QWL) programs. QWL programs aim at humanization of work and have a comprehensive vision of the work community as part of the wider society. Cherns (1975) elaborated on this vision. The basic assumptions and values implicit in the drive to improve the quality of working life maintain that autonomy is preferable to dependence and high levels of skill are preferable to low levels. Also, learning and a high degree of self-investment in work are good, provided that the work itself and the work situation offer opportunities for growth and self-realization.[1]

Newton (1978) defined the rationale for QWL programs as the need to better balance human motivation and organizational objectives in a world where changes emerge by (a) accelerating technological change; (b) shifting attitudes, life styles, and social institutions; and (c) achieving prosperity accompanied by doubts about future economic performance. In this new world of work, QWL may be viewed as an ecological factor of work, which includes the relationships among people, their organizations, and their society.

The specific configuration of a QWL program and the relative importance of its ingredients must be elaborated specifically for each organizational case and with adjustment to unique local circumstances.
Historically, however, the humanization of work and quality of working
life were often attempted by direct participation techniques, either of
the socio-technical style or the job enrichment variety. Thus, in Europe,
"Humanization of Work" programs focused on job redesign and were
developed by both unions and government. In Italy, the favorable concept was job enrichment. In France, there was the evolutionary process
of humanizing work through democratization of the work environment
and promoting improvements to working conditions. In the United
Kingdom, the humanization efforts were adjunct to collective bargaining, and the Scandinavian countries served as experimental workshops in the field of work reform.

The eclectic approach of the QWL School to participation is well exem-
plified by Kolodny and Stjernberg (1986). They studied efforts to improve
the quality of working life in three different research settings. One was a
longitudinal study of alternative work organizations in Sweden. The
second was research into new socio-technically designed plants in the
United States. The third was a study of the effects of new technology and
work organization on QWL in Sweden, Canada, and the United States.

In another project, Davis and Sullivan (1980) reported a new type of
labor- management contract involving quality of working life, based on
the Shell Sarina chemical plant in Canada. The contract provided for
union partnership in both the design of the plant and in operational
decision-making. Despite the plant's performance at nearly 200 percent
of its rated capacity, in a visit 11 years later, Davis defined the state of
the work system as "arrested development."

The observations about the socio-technical programs are generally
also valid to the QWL programs. However, there are some differences.
QWL experiments are more heterogeneous than ST projects. They
touch on work subsystems other than jobs, teams, and performance
relationships. They are more complicated because they concern
working conditions, industrial welfare, and interfaces with communities
outside the workplace, in addition to work relations.

JOB-CENTERED PROGRAMS

Perhaps the most enduring theory of job reform is that of Hackman
and Oldham (1980). They suggested redesigning and enriching jobs
with the following sufficient (but not excessive) five attributes:[2]

1. *Task variety,* which enables employees to learn and use different skills on their job and reduce the boredom and monotony on the job.
2. *Task identity,* which enables a worker to complete a whole piece of work on the job.
3. *Task significance,* which offers work contents that are important and meaningful to the jobholders.
4. *Task autonomy,* which enables employees to make decisions while doing the work and choose their way of performing the job.
5. *Task feedback,* which provides knowledge on the results of the work done and enables employees to monitor their own activities and make improvements in response.

As a matter of fact, most job enrichment programs design their activities, in part or as a whole, according to these principles. However, we cannot include job redesign in the nomenclature of participation programs when it stands alone as a single element. It gets its participative character only with other elements of work reform, such as self-managing or autonomous work groups.

GROUP-CENTERED PROGRAMS

In group-centered programs, the redesign focus is on the attributes of the traditional work group or team. Traditional work groups are continuing work units, responsible for producing goods or providing services. Their membership is typically stable, usually full-time, and is directed by supervisors who make most of the decisions about what to do, how to do it, and who does it (Cohen, 1991). Against this nonparticipatory design, Cohen and Bailey (1997) identified two types of participatory work groups: self-managing teams and parallel teams.[3]

Self-Managing Work Teams

Self-managing teams, sometimes called autonomous, semi-autonomous, self-directing, and empowered teams, are groups of employees that can self-regulate their work on relatively whole tasks. Key characteristics include (a) employees with interdependent tasks who are responsible for making a product or providing a service and (b) employee discretion over decisions such as work assignments, work methods, and scheduling of activities. Members of self-managing work teams are often trained in a variety of skills relevant to the tasks they perform (Cohen and Bailey, 1987).

Autonomous and semi-autonomous work groups were the predecessors of self-managing work groups (Wall et al., 1986), and were evolved from the socio-technical theory.[4] They are identified by a number of key features. They are small groups of co-workers (8 to 15), who share the tasks and accept responsibility for a well-defined segment of the work. They are given a high degree of discretion by the group members over such decisions as how to schedule the tasks, the allocation of jobs among the members, as well as the determination of rest breaks (Gulowsen, 1972). Also, they are rated high on other task characteristics, namely, skill, identity, significance, and feedback on the group tasks. Note that these are characteristics of the group rather than the individual job in Hackman's paradigm (Cummings, 1978).[5] Direct supervision is often unnecessary in autonomous groups. Another arrangement is to assign group leaders within the group (Jessup, 1990).

Autonomous work groups received prominence in the 1950s and 1960s, but old-style autonomous work groups are rare today. However, in a longitudinal study of semi-autonomous work groups in a large Australian heavy engineering workshop, Pearson (1992) examined, in an experimental setting, 30 groups. They were randomly categorized as autonomous or nonautonomous. The performance of these two types of work groups was evaluated in terms of job motivation, role perceptions, job satisfaction, productivity, accidents, turnover, and absenteeism. Positive changes in perceptual, affective, and behavioral responses attributable to the creation of semi-autonomous work teams were observed in autonomous groups but not in nonautonomous groups.

Self-managing teams have been a major target in the framework of work redesign for a long time. In the older bureaucratic and hierarchic work systems, teamwork has seemed almost impossible in the face of resistance to change from every corner of the organization. Nowadays, teamwork in general and self-managing or self-directing teams in particular are so abundant and common, that it is amazing to see how far the world of work has moved and how bold was the foresight of the pioneers of direct participation through autonomous groups.

Parallel Groups: Quality Circles (QC) and Employee Involvement Groups

These groups pull together people from different work units or jobs to perform functions that the regular organization is not equipped to perform well. They literally work parallel to the formal organizational structure. They generally have limited authority and can only make recommendations to management. Parallel teams are used for problem-solving and improvement-oriented activities. Examples include quality improvement teams, employee involvement groups, quality circles, and task forces.

Quality circles (QCs) have been perhaps the most prevalent parallel groups in Japan, Western Europe, the United States, and many other countries. They are small teams of volunteers (6 to12 people), not necessarily from the same work group or department, who meet regularly for about 1 hour per week (Lawler and Mohrman, 1985; Rafaeli, 1985). Through these meetings, the members can make some contribution to the decision-making processes, industrial relations, absenteeism, and turnover (Liverpool, 1990; Marks, Mirvis, Hackett, and Grady, 1986).

In practice, quality circles recommend solutions for quality and productivity problems to management. As shown in Figure 3.1, the activities of quality circles are directed toward identifying, analyzing, and solving quality-related problems in their work area and suggesting methods for improving production. It is normal for quality circles to receive training in problem solving, statistical control, and group processes (Griffin, 1988). Often the circles are implemented and assisted by a facilitator.

In the last years QCs have declined, and in many organizations the number of QC groups and the intensity of their activity have been reduced or even disappeared. Nevertheless, similar or equivalent groups for problem solving and productivity improvements with cross-departmental membership are common in many work organizations.

Participation in Quality Management Programs (TQM, CQI, BPR)

Quality management and reengineering processes are a third avenue for participation programs. However, participation is only a (desired) by-product in reengineering programs and not the main vehicle to achieve organizational goals. For example, Appelbaum and Batt (1994) made a distinction between off-the-job or "off-line" problem-solving groups of employees and management and "on-line" participation in which employees themselves make decisions about tasks or quality control on the job. For our purposes, only programs with strong participatory elements are counted in this family of direct participation pro-

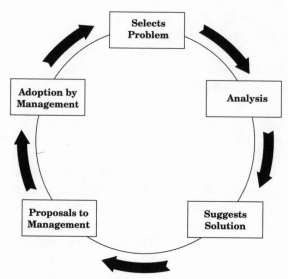

FIGURE 3.1.   *A schematic quality circle program.*

grams. Therefore, we attempt to delineate these elements in three reengineering or reform programs: total quality management (TQM), continuous quality improvement (CQI), and business process reengineering (BPR).

Total Quality Management and Continuous Quality Improvement

The total quality management (TQM) movement began with W. Edwards Deming, an American statistician who applied statistical control principles to manufacturing processes in the 1940s and started to work with Japanese companies during the 1950s. While Deming is the most well known among total quality "gurus," he is not alone. Other well-known experts include Joseph Juran, Philip Crosby, Kauro Ishikawa, and others. Today, the quality management movement has elaborated and reformulated its theoretical and practical thinking using the term *continuous quality improvement* (CQI). TQM and CQI are used interchangeably in this book. Their common ground is a system for taking action in a constantly changing environment where customer requirements are consistently met and exceeded. This system is summarized by the following principles:[6]

1. *Focus on the customer.* Products and services address the customer's needs and articulated requirements rather than those conceived by the producer or service provider.
2. *Prevention approach.* "Doing it right the first time"—instead of correcting through inspection.
3. *Management by data.* Quality improvement data include customer survey data, baseline measures of current processes, and data tracking improvements in processes and outcomes.
4. *Respect for employees at all levels.* Employees at all levels of an organization are empowered to analyze customer requirements, systematically identify opportunities for improvements, implement changes, and track the impact of these changes.
5. *Commitment to ongoing improvement.* Each time a new level of quality and customer satisfaction is reached, new improvement goals are set.
6. *Cross-functional problem solving.* Customer requirements usually call for process solutions that cut horizontally across organizational functions.
7. *Commitment to continuous quality improvement.* A commitment to CQI must be a way of life in the organization.

Organizations use many tools in realizing TQM/CQI interventions: identification of unit's customers and their priorities, providing training in flow-charting work process and in measuring system capability, generating and evaluating alternative solutions, and developing processes to support the chosen solution. These tools also employ elementary statistics to document system variability and to describe customer reactions and identify the primary sources of product and service delivery problems. They benchmark quality improvement goals and processes, conduct surveys and periodic focus groups in order to obtain information on current system capability and track changes in customer reactions, and they build interpersonal skill through training.

While TQM/CQI is not exactly the focus of this book, we will discuss the participatory aspect of quality management. As can be seen in the list above, some sort of participation is implied. However, Edosomwan (1992), a member of the Board of Examiners of the Malcolm Baldrige National Quality Award, which is the highest prize in the United States for quality management, highlighted this aspect in an eloquent way. He argued that company quality improvement could only be successful when employees have both the skills and the authority to respond to customers' needs. Employees at all levels and across all functions should be involved in the implementation of projects that can greatly improve performance. They should be included in the development of continuous improvement strategies and be given the tools and authority to make decisions and resolve problems.

Business Process Reengineering

Another variant of quality management is *business process reengineering* (BPR), and it refers to the mechanism of introducing radical rather than merely incremental change, either to a process or to an organization as a whole. Components of a BPR include a reorganization or the company's structure aimed at breaking functional hierarchies into cross-functional (horizontal) teams, implementation of a new state-of-the-art information system, and renewed efforts to refocus on the company's customers.

De Sitter et al. (1997) described a Duch variant of BPR, called Integral Organizational Renewal (IOR). The novelty of IOR has been its focus on the tension between expertise and participation. This was one of the lessons of the socio-technical experiments of the 1960s. At that time, it became evident (Mulder, 1971) that participation in situations where one party has all the expertise and the other little or none tends to increase, rather than decrease, the power distance between designers and users. The strategy chosen to deal with this paradox aims to empower system users by increasing their design expertise.

EVALUATION OF DIRECT PARTICIPATION PROGRAMS

In a polemic paper, "Far from the fad in-crowd," Lawler (1996) attempted to present a balanced assessment of the various direct participation (or Employee Involvement) programs (EIPs). He claimed that such programs had some fad-like attributes, and their mass adoption by many organizations leaves unanswered the question of whether they could and should replace the traditional bureaucratic model. Citing the study of Mohrman, Ledford, and himself, he tried to make his point.[7]

They began collecting data in 1987 from the *Fortune* 1,000 companies, and included additional data in 1990 and 1993. Their study documents both how management practices are changing and how the use of management practices is related to organizational performance. They asked companies whether and how they use self-managing teams, gainsharing schemes, training programs, and a variety of other practices that encourage involvement. They found that between 1987 and 1993 self-managed teams and knowledge-based pay showed the greatest growth. They also found a strong correlation between the adoption of employee involvement and the use of TQM practices. Financial performance among the three categories of EIP users that were researched between 1987 and 1993 is presented in the table that follows:

	Low use, %	Medium use, %	High use, %
Return on sales	6.3	8.3	10.3
Return on assets	4.7	5.8	6.9
Return on investment	9.0	11.8	14.6
Return on equity	16.6	19.7	22.8

During the mid-1980s, over 90 percent of the *Fortune* 500 U.S. companies had QC programs. Many well-regarded large companies, such as IBM, Honeywell, Digital Equipment, and Xerox, used them a lot at that time. Over 200,000 workers in the United States have been involved in these programs.

Although the adoption of quality circles has been widespread, there are many reports on a high failure rate. Goodman (1980) estimated that well over 50 percent of QC programs failed within 3 to 5 years. Lawler and Mohrman (1985) went even further and suggested that all but a few quality circle programs dwindle away after an initial productive phase. Drago (1988) indicated that out of 81 organizations involved in a quality circle program, 23 (28.4 percent) had dropped the program after an unspecified period. Within 34 firms with ongoing programs, however, he found individual circles had an 80.4 percent survival rate. Eaton (1994) found similar rates in a detailed study of two surveys in unionized settings (20 to 30 percent). She suggested that the differences between her and Drago's estimates and the earlier ones may be explained by changing historical patterns: Most of the earlier estimates relied on experience in the late 1970s or early 1980s, whereas her study and Drago's work are more recent.

Some observers pointed to the weaknesses of QC. Tang et al. (1997) summarized several reasons for QC's failure: lack of top-management support, lack of QC members' commitment, lack of problem-solving skills, QC members' turnover, lack of support from staff members, and lack of data and time.

In general, the literature suggests that self-managing teams have a modest impact on performance and the attitudes of team members

(Goodman et al., 1988). Most studies have found that self-managing teams have a direct impact on quality. For example, in the review of Pasmore et al. (1992), it was found that 100 percent of the socio-technical interventions that used self-managing team designs claimed quality improvements. Overall, the Topeka pet foods plant reported cost savings and productivity improvements (Walton, 1972). The Volvo Uddevalla plant claimed that it had achieved higher productivity than comparable plants (Kapstein and Hoerr, 1989). However, Wall et al. (1986) in their quasi-experimental study of a confectionery plant did not find productivity differences when comparing self-managing teams to traditionally managed groups. They did find cost savings as the result of fewer supervisors. Beekun's (1989) meta-analysis found that self-managing teams resulted in modest productivity improvements.

The vast majority of studies report improvements in employee satisfaction and quality of work life in self-managing team intervention. The results are inconsistent for other attitudinal indicators such as organizational commitment (Goodman et al., 1988). Finally, the effects of self-managing teams on absenteeism, safety, and health have been less systematically studied and results are inconsistent. For example, Beekun (1989) found that self-managing teams decreased absenteeism and turnover. In contrast, Cordery, Mueller, and Smith (1991) found that employees in self-managing teams have higher rates of absenteeism and turnover than their counterparts in traditional jobs.

Cohen and Bailey (1997) surveyed 24 studies of work teams (including seven studies of self-directed work teams, four studies of parallel teams, 13 studies of project teams, and 13 studies of management teams—in manufacturing, in service, in government, and in a mixture of settings). They concluded that the performance and attitudinal benefits from self-directed work teams are superior to those from parallel teams, and that autonomy is associated with higher performance for work teams, but not for project teams. In their own study of self-managing work teams, in a large U.S. telephone company, Cohen et al. (1997) showed that self-managing teams had a higher quality of working life and productivity than their traditionally managed counterparts.

The most severe criticism, however, is directed against TQM and other programs in the reengineering family. To date, most of the evidence on quality management efforts consists of anecdotal accounts of private corporations with success in implementing quality improvement processes. Largely missing are accounts of attempts at quality management that were not successful. An exception to this general state of research is the study in 1991 by the U.S. federal General Accounting Office (GAO). The GAO's study reported results of CQI interventions in 20 of the highest-scoring companies applying for the Malcolm Baldrige Award. Data covered the years of 1988 to 1990. Impressive results of improvements after adopting continuous quality techniques are presented as follows:

Decline of turnover	6.0%
Product reliability improvement	11.3%
On-time delivery improvement	4.7%
Product lead (or cycle) time reduction of	5.8%
Inventory turnover rate improvement of	7.2%
Cost of quality reduction (from lost profits, rework, and scrap)	9.0%
Customer complaint reduction of	11.6%
Market share increase of	13.7%
Sales per employee improvement of	8.6%
Return on assets increase of	1.3%

Similar claims are made by advocates of BPR, which include the achievement of high levels of savings in resources and /or time without a decrease in quality, with the following levels (Ligus, 1993): 35 percent reduction in the cost of sales; 80 percent reduction in delivery time; 80 percent reduction in inventories, and 70 percent reduction in the cost of delivering quality.

However, some consultants argued that quality management approaches such as CQI and BPR tend to come into vogue during periods of economic recession only to disappear from the scene in times of economic recovery, as organizations that are not so profitable rehire people who can be carried during boom times (Rigby, 1993). Surveys indicated a high failure rate of BPR programs. Hammer and Champy (1993) estimated that between 50 and 70 percent of organizations that undertook BPR failed. Pollalis (1996) summarized the reasons for high failure rates of BPR programs: lack of management commitment and leadership, resistance to change, unclear specifications, inadequate resources, technocentrism, a lack of user and/or customer involvement, and failure to address the human aspect of planned change. The similarity with Tang et al.'s (1997) conclusions is striking.

Grant, Shani, and Krishnan (1994) argued that the assumptions and theories underlying quality management are incompatible with the

American model and practice of the firm. TQM was developed by industrial engineers and was based on statistical theory, while conventional management practices are developed at leading business schools and based on economic theory. Also, middle management and smaller companies have disseminated TQM, while new innovations in U.S. management practices are usually developed and disseminated from the top down by leading industrial companies. TQM requires major changes in management practices, including work and organizational redesign, a redefinition of managerial roles, and changes in organizational goals. In contrast to TQM, with its primary objective of customer satisfaction, maximization of profit of shareholders takes priority in the U.S. model of the firm. The top-down strategic planning, financial control systems, and asset management tied to the economic model, inevitably, are in conflict with quality improvement in production operations and bottom-up change.

Oren Harari (1997) added that only about one-fifth, at best one-third, of TQM programs in the United States and Europe have achieved significant or even tangible improvements in quality, productivity, competitiveness, or financial returns. However, we are interested here mainly in the participatory aspect of the quality management practices. From this point of view, Richard Hackman and Ruth Wageman (1995) suggested a profound and balanced assessment of TQM. Among other things, they examined behavioral processes associated with TQM across four issues:

1. *Design of work.* A quality team is usually quite well designed from the point of view of work motivation. However, this is not the case for ordinary front-line employees for whom there is no adequate motivational structure in most TQM programs.

2. *Extrinsic motivation.* According to TQM philosophy, extrinsic rewards, including pay, should not be contingent on individual or team performance. However, this principle is unrealistic over the longer term. Workers may be proud and satisfied in their contributions to the organization in the initial stage of a TQM project. However, in the longer run they will demand their monetary share as the fruits of their contributions.

3. *Opportunities for learning.* Employees are encouraged to find better ways to accomplish their work. However, once something has been discovered that improves work practices, then that improvement is identified as a best practice that everyone is expected to follow. This can confuse employees as to the value of learning, and when learning should be set aside in favor of performing.

4. *Locus of authority.* This is the dilemma of empowerment in TQM programs. Empowering members to be full participants, who should be
actively involved in analyzing and solving problems, conflicts with the
traditional hierarchic authority structure, which, according to the TQM
philosophy, is unchanged.

Quality management techniques touch upon very important ingredients of direct participation of employees in their job or their work
groups. However, these techniques can be very unparticipatory and
undemocratic.

NOTES

1. Cherns (1975) did not overlook the weaknesses of the QWL
approach—ignoring power relations within work organizations and undermining class struggle and labor power.

2. Herzberg et al. (1959), much earlier, argued that because organizations
employ whole persons, it is important to pay attention to human needs beyond
the required skills for task performance, which are dictated by technology.
These needs include some control over the material and processes, some task
variety, opportunity for learning, and the need to have interesting and meaningful work.

3. They identified other types of work teams, not necessarily participatory
ones: project teams and management teams. Project teams are time-limited and
produce one-time outputs, such as a new product or service. For the most part,
project team tasks are nonrepetitive in nature and involve considerable application of knowledge, judgment, and expertise. Frequently, project teams draw
their members from different disciplines and functional units, so that special-
ized expertise can be applied to the project at hand. When a project is completed, the members either return to their functional units or move on to the
next project. Management teams coordinate and provide direction to the sub-
units under their jurisdiction, laterally integrating interdependent sub-units
across key business processes. A management team is responsible for the
overall performance of a business unit. Its authority stems from the hierarchical
rank of its members (Herzberg et al., 1959).

4. Emery (1980) makes the distinction between semi-autonomous groups
and self-managing groups. The former are granted authority for decision-
making, but may lack the necessary infrastructure, such as an effective information system that enables true self-management (Pasmore, 1995).

5. Some researchers played with the idea of integration with job-charac-
teristics theory. However, there has been limited evidence to support the

claimed effects of job enrichment in autonomous work groups (Wall et al., 1986; Pasmore, 1995).

6.   The TQM/CQI literature is vast. The summary is adapted from "A Plan for Continuous Improvement," University of Maryland at College Park, 1991.

7.   Interested readers will find a balanced evaluation of Lawler et al.'s project by Konczak (1996).

Chapter 4

Economic Participation Programs

Prominent examples of the older type of economic participation are employee suggestion schemes (ESS), which were forerunners of the contemporary gainsharing programs, designed to elicit new ideas, save money, and yield substantial rewards to employees who contribute worthwhile suggestions. ESSs are rooted in both industry and public administration. One of the first major programs was that of Eastman Kodak, a system going into effect in 1898 when workers received compensation of $2 for their suggestions. In the middle of the twentieth century, the most well-known ESS was the Scanlon Plan, developed from the innovative work of Joseph Scanlon during the 1940s and 1950s.

A steelworker and union leader during the Depression, Scanlon concluded that a company's health, indeed its very survival, required a climate of cooperation between labor and management, rather than rivalry and competition. As a staff member of the United Steelworkers of America, he used his ideas to improve productivity, thereby saving organizations and jobs. His work came to the attention of Douglas McGregor at the Massachusetts Institute of Technology, where he was invited to join the faculty. Together, McGregor and Scanlon pioneered the concept of employee involvement. The early "Scanlon Plans" included a monthly cash bonus to all employees when labor costs were reduced below that of historical base periods. Unfortunately, Scanlon died prematurely in 1956 and never realized the impact he had on world industry. Upon his death, Carl Frost at Michigan State University became one of the most influential and dedicated Scanlon practitioners.

Frost refined Scanlon's ideas into four fundamental principles: Identity and Education, Participation and Responsibility, Equity and Accountability, and Competence and Commitment. The underlying idea was to create organizational effectiveness while promoting individual growth and responsibility.

Even in the last decade, ESSs have been widely used. The National Association of Suggestion Systems (NASS), an American nonprofit group, surveyed its 900 members in 1989 and found that nearly one million employee suggestions had been received through company ESSs. The respondents further indicated that more than 32 percent of those suggestions were adopted, for total cost savings of at least $2 billion. However, most of the Scanlon-type programs nowadays are classified under the rubric of gain-sharing programs, which are discussed in the following section.

PROFIT SHARING AND GAINSHARING

There are three forms of economic participation programs: profit sharing, gainsharing, and employee stock ownership (Cooke, 1994; Dar-El, 1986). The differences between profit sharing and gainsharing are in the criteria used in making bonus calculations, in the timing of bonus calculations, and in payments. Bonuses received under profit sharing are based on profits, typically calculated annually, semi-annually, or quarterly. Bonuses received under gainsharing, on the other hand, are based on measures of performance other than profits (for example, on reductions in costs that might include labor, materials, or overhead costs, or on improvements in quality and/or safety, scrap reduction, and so on).

A recurrent issue is whether participation of workers in ownership or in profits should be included as a type of participation program. In their classic book, Flanders, Pomeranz and Woodward (1968), who studied the British partnership of John Lewis, concluded (and Clarke et al. [1972] and Blumberg [1968] reached the same conclusion) that on the workplace level there was no correlation between profit and/or stock sharing, on the one hand, and power sharing and industrial democracy, on the other.

Various forms of ownership democratization in work organizations tend to change the membership status of employees dramatically, and may induce significant psychological and attitudinal changes on their part. However, the question is whether distribution of some ownership rights will change the basic submissive role of workers versus management roles. For example, the current popularity of Employee Stock Ownership Programs (ESOP), which is discussed below, again raises the question whether it facilitates industrial democracy and employee participation. Rooney (1988) found that employee influence over decisions in U.S. firms was slightly more pronounced in employee-owned firms than in conventional firms. Also in the United Kingdom, Pendelton et al. (1994) found that establishment of an ESOP made little difference regarding the intensity of employee participation. Occasionally, the development of industrial democracy is possible in those cases where employees or their representatives play a dominant role in the creation of an ESOP. The novelty of employee participation in those ESOPs where meaningful extensions of industrial democracy are secured is that participation is primarily directed at strategic rather than day-to-day or task-related decisions. This is plainly at odds with developments in employee participation since the end of the 1970s (Ramsay, 1991), and is rather surprising, in view of the fact that most of the research in the field (partly cited even in this book) has found that the widespread innovations are at the task and work group rather than at the strategic level.

The fundamental assumption underlying economic participation is that if employees' earnings are tied to performance, they will adjust their effort to increase income (Weitzman and Kruse, 1990). Also, if these performance-related payments are group-based incentives, the monitoring costs associated with supervisory control will be reduced (Kruse, 1993). Economic participation presumably and indirectly increases employee effort and commitment by improving information about company performance, by educating employees about the connection between their earnings, profitability, and organizational effectiveness (Mitchell et al., 1990).

However, a number of factors operate to reduce gains. First, there is the "free rider" or employee-shirking problem, whereby some employees will merely take unfair advantage of group-generated performance gains and their consequent bonuses. Levine and Tyson (1990) argued, though, that group-based incentives induce employees to monitor the behavior of coworkers and impose social sanctions on those employees who shirk complying with cooperative work group norms. Second, employees may be reluctant to exchange some fixed earnings for variable earnings, because of the higher risks attached to the latter (Weitzman and Kruse, 1990).

Further, the strength or magnitude of the potential effects of group-based incentives is likely to be moderated by the specific incentive formulas and the timing of bonus payments. First, what employees accomplish in their respective work areas is apt to be only imperfectly correlated with overall company profits. Although the bonuses provided by gain-sharing formulas are more directly tied to actual employee effort than are bonuses based on profits, employees still may not reap the full benefit of improved production performance. Any drop in the sales value of the product or increase in materials costs caused by market forces beyond the control of the work force would offset some of the gain achieved by reducing labor and other costs.

Second, most profit-sharing bonus schedules defer payments, often as promised pension endowments. Gain-sharing bonuses, on the other hand, are typically paid every several weeks. Given the greater frequency and timeliness of gain-sharing bonuses in comparison to profit-sharing bonuses, it seems likely that they provide workers with a stronger incentive to be more productive (Eaton and Voos, 1992). Nevertheless, assuming that employees are not so myopic as to completely reject the value of retirement income (received at more favorable tax rates), even deferred profit sharing can influence work-related behavior.

Florkowski (1987) proposed a profit-sharing model which assumes that companies establish profit-sharing programs in response to internal and/or market-based circumstances. Another study by Florkowski and Schuster (1992) of 160 participants from three companies that implemented profit-sharing programs demonstrates that perceptions of pay equity and fairness in the performance-reward system were key factors in generating participant support for the plan.

Research findings on gainsharing often indicate that the expected improvements in productivity, satisfaction, and commitment in organizations with a Scanlon-type plan are quite modest. Collins (1996) identified three groups of participants in a gain-sharing program: supporters, opponents, and neutrals. Supporters regarded gainsharing as a beneficial change for the organization and/or themselves. Opponent managers were skeptical about gainsharing. They felt threatened, fearing that gainsharing would empower nonmanagement employees whom they consider untrustworthy or unqualified for this responsibility. Opponent workers and other nonmanagement employees were skeptical about managers' intentions because of negative experience with managers. Neutrals did not intentionally undermine the change, nor did they try actively to facilitate the change.

Collins explained how a gain-sharing plan failed after 6 years, despite many beneficial outcomes to the organization, the work groups, and the individuals. The lessons may be relevant to other participation programs: Management was not sincere and consistent in support of the program. Middle managers and professional experts sabotaged the process because they feared for their traditional position. Employees who supported the program enjoyed their new power in the program and were less interested in the monetary bonuses. Neutrals tended to lose faith in the program when they felt that managers abused the gain-sharing principles and procedures, and opponent employees at the outset were interested only in the bonus and not in power sharing, because they did not believe that they could get any power.

The experience with profit-sharing and gain-sharing programs teaches us that remunerative participation is another way of participation—though not a perfect alternative. It is neither simpler nor cheaper to manage, and the motivational assumptions of these programs still have to compete with other assumptions about the human nature of employees and their willingness to contribute to their workplace.

EMPLOYEE STOCK OWNERSHIP PROGRAMS (ESOPs)

The idea of employee stock ownership was suggested by Louis Kelso, a San Francisco financier and corporate lawyer, in his book, written with Patricia Hetterer and entitled *The Two Factor Theory — The Economics of Reality* (1967). His basic idea was to create new owners through the use of production credit. The employee stock ownership program and similar financial mechanisms provide access to productive credit for employees who normally do not have such access. The innovation of ESOPs is that employees acquire individual shares on credit, without any cash payment or salary deduction on their part. The credit is repaid over a number of years through the increased revenue of the company and the employees pay for their shares through increased productivity. The employees receive their shares upon retirement, but from the first year obtain dividends on their shares if the company shows a profit. The U.S. Congress has passed over 20 acts containing provisions that encourage employee ownership.[1]

ESOPs are a relatively new phenomenon, which have experienced amazing growth in the United States. From 1974 to 1995 over 11 million U.S. employees have become part owners through ESOPs of over 11,000 corporations, including some of the largest in the United States, with $150 billion in corporate stock. About 1,000 of these publicly held companies have at least 4 percent employee ownership, with an average of over 12 percent.[2] A variety of ESOPs, including famous examples like United Airlines, Procter and Gamble, and General Mills, have generated significant employee ownership. Their programs generally emerged in the midst of takeovers, as the result of big restructuring and crises in the 1970s and the 1980s. But in the 1990s, employee ownership took on a different character. There were fewer ESOPs in public takeovers and a lot of new employee ownership.

U.S. experience indicates that participation arrangements vary widely between ESOPs: Relatively few have developed forms of corporate governance, such as employee representatives on the company board, and many have no voting rights on shares held in trust. A rather greater number have expanded participation at the individual or task-related level (General Accounting Office, 1987). The reasons for establishing ESOPs also vary: Many are established to provide pension funds, some to block hostile takeovers, and only a small number to advance industrial democracy (Klein and Rosen, 1986). However, those establishing an ESOP for democratic reasons are likely to introduce more advanced participative structures than those creating an ESOP for pension planning.

Pendleton et al. (1994) assessed the potential of ESOP for industrial democracy based on the British example, but their analysis is also valid for other countries. Despite their comparatively small numbers in the United Kingdom, there are some features associated with ESOP firms that make them of interest to participation programs. Whereas conventional share schemes do not lead to the creation of new institutions of employee participation, ESOPs are a potentially democratic form of financial participation. Since shares are usually held collectively before payments are made to individual employees, ESOPs can transform ownership into employees' control. However, the extent to which ESOPs fulfill the apparent option of greater industrial democracy depends on other factors, which are likely to affect the extent of employee participation in practice.

Again, it is not enough to distribute ownership rights. To attain real participation, work organizations have to build and maintain opportunity structures for personal and collective sharing of power and responsibility, and the workforce needs to have the will and skill to participate effectively.

NOTES

1.   It is also important to note what the ESOP is not. The ESOP is not any kind of collective ownership, cooperativism, syndicalism (ownership by trade unions), or the German "co-determination" model (union representation on the company board), or the Yugoslav "workers' management" model (politically driven management). The ESOP results in private-sector, profit-maximizing corporations, in which a large number of their own employees and other citizens have individual share ownership.

2.   In the United Kingdom, the ESOP concept was developed in the mid-1980s. It was created in the motorway services station organization Roadchef in 1987 when a quarter of the company's equity was purchased by an Employee Benefits Trust with the help of a loan from the trade union bank Unity Trust. Since then the development of ESOPs has been associated primarily with the government's privatization program. Today, there are some 300 ESOPs in the United Kingdom.

Part II

Two Generations of Participation Programs

Historians may trace many properties of participation programs as early as the first decades of the twentieth century. For example, the roots of the German Works Council can be traced as far back as the end of World War I and the Works Council Act of 1920. This was also the time of the Whitely committees, as a form of consultative participation in Great Britain. However, participation as an issue on the national agenda emerged only after World War II. My bias is based on the conspicuous difference between what I call two generations of participation programs after World War II: the first decades of workers' participation programs and the last decades of employee involvement programs.

Chapter 5

Workers' Participation: The First Generation

During the 1960s and 1970s, many countries with different political regimes and levels of economic development, like Great Britain, Yugoslavia, West Germany, Poland, Norway, Algeria, and India, experienced various programs of workers' participation. Strauss and Rosenstein (1970) attributed this convergence around the idea of workers' participation to the common expectations that this idea would serve as a panacea to a wide range of human and managerial problems at the workplace level. In those years and in many countries, managers, union and political leaders, administrators, and social thinkers recognized signs and symptoms of discontent at all levels of the workforce— blue collar workers, white collar employees, professionals, managers, not merely low-paid and underprivileged workers.[1]

INDUSTRIAL PEACE AND PRODUCTIVITY

The first decades after World War II were characterized by economic growth, a fast increase in standards of living in many countries, high hopes and an optimistic view of the future, and expectations for more freedom and more democracy in international relations, as well as domestic affairs. Labor parties and labor unions had never been stronger or more influential. They could move from legitimacy and recognition battles to other strategic issues, namely, job security and improvement of standards of living *and* working. Employers faced full-employment economies with a better-educated and organized work-force. What they needed in the first place were industrial peace and high productivity in order to supply the high and growing demand for goods and services. Industrial democracy and workers' participation (mainly in indirect and representative configurations) seemed an attractive solution to both labor and capital leaders.

SOCIO-TECHNICAL WORK REFORM AND HUMANIZATION OF WORK LIFE

Although most of the participation experience in the first generation is of indirect representative programs, we have to remark on the socio-technical movement in Europe, which dated back to the 1950s, and which had a profound impact on direct participation programs in the second generation. The background of the socio-technical movement was the prosperous years of the first generation, which witnessed rapid increase in the training and education levels of the workforce. This caused a gap between the capabilities and ambitions of workers on the one hand and the monotonous and degrading work in mass manufacturing and offices on the other hand. The consequences were high levels of worker turnover and absenteeism and other symptoms of escapism, as well as decreased productivity and quality of products and services (Hertog, 1977). A number of large European firms, including Philips, Olivetti, Volvo, Saab, VW, and Renault, were looking for alternatives to the mechanistic work systems. However, the almost unintended beginning was in the Tavistock Institute of Human Relations in London and in some British coal mines, and later on in Norway and Sweden.

In 1949, Eric Trist, from the Tavistock Institute, and Fred Emery, an Australian social scientist, joined Ken Bamforth, a trade unionist and a former coal miner, to study mining practices in England. They noticed a new interesting development in coal mining. Technical improvements in roof control had made it possible to mine "short wall" and to reorganize the labor process. Instead of each miner being responsible for a separate task in the mechanized "long wall" mining, workers organized autonomous groups that rotated tasks and shifts among themselves with minimum supervision. This new reorganization enabled the miners to renew a tradition of small group autonomy and responsibility that had been dominant in the days before mechanization.

The theoretical and practical collaboration of Emery and Trist and others over the next several decades resulted in what has become known as the *socio-technical systems approach*. In 1962 Emery and Trist were invited by Einar Thorsrud of the Technical University in Oslo to participate in the Norwegian Industrial Democracy Project—a joint labor-management endeavor to enhance workers' control. The insights of their field experiments in participatory work redesign spread to Sweden and other European countries. Other well-known Tavistock-initiated socio-technical projects were in India, in the calico weaving mills in Ahmadabad, led by Rice (1958), and in a program, led by Herbst, in the design of work in the Norwegian ship *M/S Balao*.

QUALITY OF WORKING LIFE

I already referred to the years of full employment and prosperity of the 1960s and early 1970s. These years provided fertile soil for ideas about quality of working life, industrial democracy, workplace welfare programs, and design of better jobs and working conditions. This agenda was suggested to face the decline of work ethics among the young and more educated employees, and to meet their expectations for meaningful work, equity, and a decent human workplace.

The quality of working life (QWL) movement in the 1970s combined ideas and practices from both the socio-technical tradition and the human relations tradition. Several programs of "Quality of Working Life" or "Humanization of Work" were widely popular throughout the industrialized world. These programs were sought to restore industrial peace within the enterprise and to reduce manifestations of workers' discontent and frustration (and their economic costs). Emphasis was placed on humanization of the content of work or improvement of the quality of working life.[2]

Nevertheless, most of the workers' participation programs until the 1970s were of the indirect representative type. In the European countries, the relative lack of union interest in direct participation programs was consistent with the centralized labor relations systems that prevailed for most of the postwar period. Such centralized systems involved a trade-off: Employers (and governments) accepted union participation on national and industrial levels of policy-making in return for union consent to management prerogatives in running the local enterprises.

The economic and social tensions of the late 1960s and early 1970s, however, led unions in several industrialized countries (Federal Republic of Germany, Italy, and Sweden) to pay greater attention to direct participation strategies. For example, in 1974, the German unions and the federal German government launched a Humanization of Working Life Program. In Italy, a similar initiation was started in the early 1970s in the automobile industry, and, in Sweden, legislative reforms were promoted to enhance participation of unions in decision-making on technological change and work organization (Ozaki, 1996).

NOTES

1.   In the United States, these feelings were the trigger for the Nixon administration's task force on Work in America, which was a milestone in work reforms in America. Typical studies that document the spirit of the time among the U.S. labor force can be found in the book of readings by Gruneberg (1976) and the popular study by Sheppard and Herrick (1972).

2.   On practical efforts to address the humanization and participation ideas in the 1970s, see the two-volume book by Davis and Cherns (1975).

Chapter 6

Major Players of Workers' Participation

In the first generation, the main arena of participation programs was in Europe. The experiences of three countries with indirect representative participation had a unique impact on many other countries: joint consultation in the United Kingdom, co-determination in Germany, and self-management in the former Yugoslavia. To this list of major players in the first generation of participation programs, I add the Scandinavian version of workers' participation and the collective bargaining model of North America as a possible variant of representative workers' participation.

GREAT BRITAIN: JOINT CONSULTATION

In the United Kingdom, the popular form of participation, in addition to collective bargaining, was joint consultation between management and employees. This arrangement evolved in World War I in the public sector, as an emergency forum for information exchange about productivity, wages, and labor relations between employers and employees in various forms of works councils, known as Whitley Committees. Later on, these consultative councils spread to the private sector as well. They were active and popular for a couple of decades. However, after World War II, they declined and, with the rise of the shop steward movement, most of the committees ceased to exist (Emery and Thorsrud, 1969, 52–53).

After the war, Britain nationalized several key industries, such as the coal mines and the railways. In the nationalized enterprises, employees could be represented on the boards of directors. However, the labor representatives were forced to leave their positions in the unions. In the private sector, employers and unions were against any form of joint consultation, and preferred to include any participatory arrangement in the framework of collective bargaining. This was also the recommendation of the important Donovan royal committee on industrial relations in Britain in 1966. This general antiparticipation climate characterized the United Kingdom until recently. Another well-known royal committee issued the Bullock report on industrial democracy in 1977, revealing a sign of change. In this report the major recommendation was to revise the British company law, in order to adopt co-determination arrangements in accordance with continental Europe of that time. However, this initiative was curtailed for many years immediately after the rise of the new conservative government of Margaret Thatcher in 1979.

However, in some public companies and in several private companies, such as Glaciers Metals, Scott-Bader, and John Louis, there was a long tradition of joint consultation and economic participation. King and van de Vall (1969, 165) portrayed a model of a British joint consultation scheme (Figure 6.1). The important distinction in the model is between authority relations and consultative relations. There is a clear asymmetry in these relationships, where employees are entitled to be consulted on some issues, but management has the right to decide.

Joint consultation schemes that survived in the United Kingdom in the 1960s and 1970s were able to maintain regular meetings and to meet the requirements of their bylaws. The general attitudes toward the program among the members of the consultative works councils were positive. However, rank-and-file employees were less positive about the scheme. In some cases, the works councils weakened the local shop stewards or antagonized the union officials. In other cases, members in works councils withdrew from participation because they felt that management refrained from consulting on major issues and offered trivial agenda items for the council's meetings. In the nationalized companies, the works councils were exposed to another pressure—in some cases they were accused of being too close to management at the expense of the British taxpayers.

GERMANY: CO-DETERMINATION

The development of the co-determination system in West Germany after World War II into a full-fledged system of workers' participation, began as a socio-political buffer against a potential coalition between the captains of the German industry and the ultra-right forces in post-war Germany. It was also meant to involve the German labor movement in the recovery of Germany by proposing a democratic program to reorganize German industry (Emery and Thorsrud, 1969, 42–44). The idea of co-determination, however, appeared in Germany earlier in 1920 in the Works Councils Act, which prescribed works councils for all establishments with at least 20 workers. In the 1922 amendment to this law, employees were entitled to information disclosure on the company's business state and the works councils were able to elect representatives to the company's management organs (Co-determination in the Federal Republic of Germany, June 1980, 9–10). Today the participation system is exercised through two major channels: in supervisory boards of business companies, and through works councils.

Supervisory Boards

In medium-sized or large companies (stock corporations, limited liability companies, partnerships limited by shares, cooperatives, or mutual insurance companies), employees can influence company policy through their representatives on the supervisory boards. This arrangement of the supervisory board extends to all company activities. Thus the supervisory board, for instance, appoints the members of the

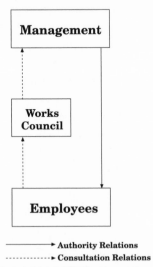

FIGURE 6.1. *A schematic joint consultation program.* (Adapted from King and van de Vall, 1978.)

management board. It may also revoke their appointments, demand information on all company matters, and have the last word on important business decisions, e.g., with regard to major investments or rationalization measures.

In iron, coal, and steel companies that employ more than 1,000 employees, labor representatives are equal in numbers to shareholders' appointees on the company's supervisory board, and there is another neutral member. Enterprises other than iron, coal, and steel companies that either alone or together with their subsidiaries have a workforce of more than 2,000 are governed by the Co-determination Act of 1976, which requires that the supervisory board be made up of equal numbers of representatives of shareholders and employees. However, the shareholders have a slight advantage in the event of a stalemate in that the chairman of the supervisory board, who is always a representative of the shareholders, has a second casting and decisive vote.

Some of the labor seats on the supervisory board are reserved for the unions represented in the company (or group): two in the case of a 12-member or 16-member board and three in the case of a 20-member board. All labor members on the supervisory board, i.e., those on the company's payroll and the union representatives, are elected by direct ballot or by delegates.

Shareholder representatives on the supervisory board are elected at the firm's shareholders' meeting. The members of the supervisory board elect the chairman and deputy chairman at their constituent meeting. A two-thirds majority is required. Failing this, a second vote is taken in which the shareholder representatives elect the chairman and the labor representatives elect the deputy chairman.

The supervisory board appoints the members of the management board and may also revoke their appointment. Here, too, a two-thirds majority is necessary; otherwise a mediation committee is appointed. A labor director with equal rights is chosen according to the same procedure. The labor director is chiefly concerned with personnel and social affairs. In the appointment of a labor director, the employees' representatives have no veto. (see Figure 6.2)

Works Council

The works council is entitled to full and timely information rights on the current and projected economic situation of the firm. These rights were reinforced as a result of the 1989 amendments to the Works Constitution Act of 1972. Also, clearly defined consultation rights are supplied and are applied to planned structural changes to the plant and prospective changes in equipment and working methods that affect job requirements, all decisions relating to manpower planning and individual dismissals. (see Figure 6.3)

The works councils represent the entire workforce, and are formally independent of unions. In practice, however, Addison et al. (1996) reported that the majority of candidates are not only union members but also union nominees. They cited results for works council elections in the mid-nineties, where 73.5 percent of councilors were union members at a time when union membership comprised approximately 35 percent of the working population. In the 1990s, the ties between the works councils and the unions were closer than ever. Cooperation between unions and works councils is fostered by workers' education programs conducted by the union movement, and by their joint presence on the supervisory boards of companies. Most councilors are union members, and in that capacity they may also serve on union bargaining committees. In some works agreements in large enterprises, works councils regulate matters that fall outside legally defined areas (Mueller-Jentsch 1995, 60–61).

The German experience in the first three decades after World War II can be summarized in four points (Emery and Thorsrud, 1969, 44–52; Adams and Rummel, 1977; Hartman, 1970; Wilpert, 1975):

1. The participation institutions (the co-determination and the works councils) were stable and worked well.
2. Although conflicts of interest between the unions and the works councils did not materialize as originally feared, friction existed because of the obscured demarcation of powers between the two institutions.

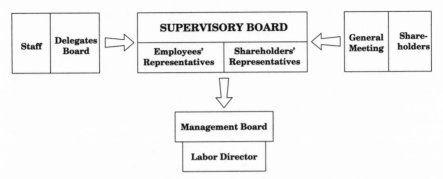

FIGURE 6.2. *German codertermination. (The 1976 Act).* (Adapted from Co-determination in the Federal Republic of Germany, June 1980.)

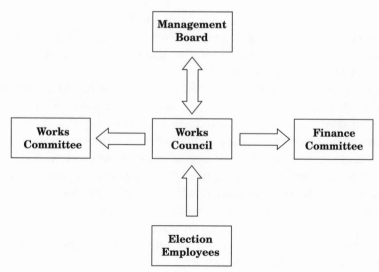

FIGURE 6.3. *German works council (1972 Act).* (Adapted from Co-determination in the Federal Republic of Germany, June 1980.)

3. Most experts accept positive assessment of the association between the participation institutions and industrial peace and prosperity in West Germany in that time. However, they could not ascertain the causal relationships. Attitude surveys showed that there was a general positive attitude toward the system. However, most employees were indifferent and only the labor activists were enthusiastic, many of whom used the participation opportunities to develop their own careers in union and management roles.

Since the golden age of the German co-determination institutions in the 1970s, the public mood has changed. Hans-Olaf Henkel, president of the Federation of German Industry said: "This thing that we celebrated 20 years ago [the 1976 law that ensures a parity of worker representation] is not making it." (*International Herald Tribune,* June 30, 1997).

Previously, German captains of industry would not dare to call the co-determination system into doubt in a country where it is practically sacrosanct. Moreover, the German labor movement consistently rejected the slightest encroachment on their right to elect half of the members of a company's board of supervisors. But Henkel was insistent that the system is flawed and impedes the global competitive edge of Germany. To support his argument, Henkel said that there is not a single country in the world that adopts the German co-determination system. He also assessed that two decades of co-determination have shown that it can impede decision-making, delay restructuring, block divestitures, and suppress boardroom debate.

FitzRoy and Kraft (1985, 1987, 1990) supported this view of the works councils, namely, that they hinder efficient resource allocation, reduce profitability, and undermine flexibility - all of which are essential for innovation and modern technology; and in addition they blame the works councils for creating excessive bureaucratization. However, in a careful study, Addison et al. (1996) criticized FitzRoy and Kraft's study for its methodology, data quality, and interpretations. They examined the effect of works councils on profitability and innovation. They found, contrary to earlier reports, that only 20 percent of firms have works councils. However, works councils are universal in all firms with 1,000 or more employees. They found negative correlation between the presence of works councils and firm profitability, but not with innovative activity. Therefore, they concluded that works councils are bad for profits but, by the same token, there is no negative spillover to other dimensions of firm performance.

In a recent project discussed in the book The German Model of Codetermination and Co-operative Governance, Bertelsmann Foundation/Hans-Bockler Foundation (eds.) (Gutersloh 1998), the assessment of the German system in the 1990s is summarized in the following main points:

1. German co-determination has contributed to cooperation between employers and employees based on mutual trust, primarily by statutorily underpinning the participation rights of the workforce.
2. Co-determination has adapted in a differentiated way to the specific technical and economic circumstances. This has led in practice to highly differentiated forms of co-determination, underpinned by a uniform legal basis. In day-to-day practice, co-determination has proved able, often to an astounding degree, to adapt to new circumstances in plants and companies undergoing change by means of a diverse, improvised, and innovative development of institutions and procedures to meet the needs of the situation at hand. Examples include the delegation of works councils; co-determination rights to work and project groups; an appropriate distribution of competencies among plant, company, and group-level works councils; and the application of the "spirit" of company co-determination laws to new corporate structures that were no longer adequately covered by existing law. The numerous efforts observed in practice to render co-

determination more flexible, less bureaucratic, and more highly decentralized, reflecting the new economic, technological, and organizational conditions, deserve the support of government, the social partners, and the labor courts.

3. Nevertheless, new forms of employment and corporate organization threaten the value of co-determination. The increasing importance for employment at small and medium-sized enterprises, in which there is no works councils, or at least no full-time employee representative, leads to a loss of importance and influence of co-determination as a whole.

4. In the past, co-determination has repeatedly and successfully adjusted to changes in competitive conditions. It now must face the challenge of increasing cost pressure, new innovation requirements, shortened decision-making times, and more demanding investors in the context of increasingly globalized goods and capital markets.

5. Co-determination on the supervisory board is particularly controversial. Representatives of industry have argued for a reduction in the size of co-determined supervisory boards in order to enable them to work more efficiently. Representatives of labor, on the other hand, are in favor of maintaining the number of supervisory board members stipulated by law, in order to ensure that greater expertise is brought into the company. There is agreement, however, on the urgent need to simplify the procedures for elections to the supervisory board under the 1976 Co-determination Act.

Mueller (1999) reminded us that in Germany there is a dual system, with collective agreements (negotiated between unions and employers) and plant-level agreements (negotiated between works councils and management). This system possesses considerable built-in flexibility and is open to new ideas. This was also the conclusion of the Bertelsmann Foundation and the Hans-Bockler Foundation's study. Co-determination was no longer a state affair, but rather an element of single organizations within society that required further development. Mueller believed that this dual system is not necessarily in conflict with the new flexible methods of management. On the contrary, they can work well together to solve problems such as how to reconcile the security that workers want with the flexibility companies need. It seems that in countries like Denmark, Germany, Ireland, Netherlands, and Belgium, where managements accept greater participation, employee representatives also desire it. Thus, employers' preference for direct forms of participation and the indirect participation favored by trade unions, such as collective bargaining, joint consultation, or co-determination, are converging.

YUGOSLAVIA: SELF-MANAGEMENT

The self-management system in the former Yugoslavia was created after World War II around the popular committees and works councils that were established to run the economy during the war. After the war, the Yugoslavs, under victorious Tito, attempted to lead a liberalized economy in a communist framework, which would mark an independent model of socialism and would weaken the dependency on the Stalinist Soviet Union. The Yugoslav system also had to face the unique circumstances of the multi-ethnic, multi-national, and geographically diversified nature of the country (Blumberg, 1968, chap. 8). The central idea of self-management was to transfer responsibilities and authorities to employees, and gradually to release the central planning and control of the state. These principles had been anchored in the Yugoslav constitution and laws since 1950, and were re-amended in 1962, 1967, 1971, 1974, and 1976. (Emery and Thorsrud, 1969, 42–31; Stambuk, 1985; and Mirkovic, 1987)

The Yugoslav work organizations were owned both de jure and de facto not by state or private owners, but rather by a social self-government institution called "social ownership" (*drustveno vlasnistvo*). Accordingly, resources, productive capacities, and capital goods were owned by the society. Thus, while Yugoslav workers could vote on what to do with profits, they were technically working for the good of the society (Witt, 1992).

Participation in this system consisted of direct participation and personal attendance at the meetings of all the workers and employees of a workplace who could take part in the debate and the decision-making procedure, directly by a referendum in which all workers may vote, and indirectly through the works councils. The works council held the highest authority in the enterprise (with membership between 15 and 120, depending on the workforce size). The council was elected directly by all manual and other employees for a 2- or 3-year term. The council and the popular committee (a local community and the Communist party organ) nominated the enterprise director—often an outside expert, who selected the management team. Officially, the works council monitored the management team and the director, and it was enhanced by consulting organs, such as the local Communist

League, suppliers, creditors, and governmental authorities (Abrahamsson, 1977, chap. 13). (see Figure 6.4.)

At the first international conference on participation and self-management, Pusic and Supek (1972, Vol. 1, 6–7), two prominent Yugoslav researchers, summarized the Yugoslav experience with self-management in the 1960s:

1. In the 1960s there were many works councils in all the economic sectors, and their position as a recognized institution was strengthened and stabilized. Nevertheless, workers were less interested in the details of management and more concerned with their own private position and rewards in their workplace.

2. Research studies showed that during that time (the 1960s), there was still a gap between the desired and actual power sharing in the enterprise. In the apex of the hierarchy of power were first the managers, then the works council, then the work supervisors, and, finally, the rank-and-file workers. The desired order of the power hierarchy was works council at the top, then management and the rank and file, and supervisors at the bottom.

3. The works councils had, in a decreasing order, influence on wages and salaries, social benefits expenses, investments, accommodations for

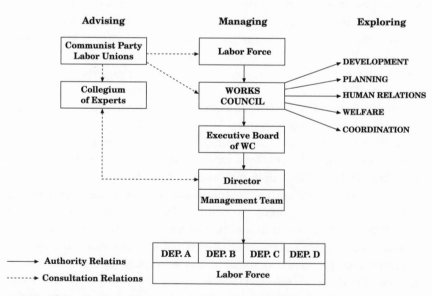

FIGURE 6.4. *A schematic Yugoslav self-management program.* (Adapted from King and van de Vall, 1978.)

workers, replacement of equipment, personnel decisions, production planning, and organizational merges.

4. The self-management was more successful, according to workers' assessments, in smaller and newer enterprises, in enterprises with simpler technology, and among male, older, educated, skilled, and more politically active workers.

5. Self-management was weaker in governmental and administrative organizations and stronger in functional and professional organizations. Also, citizens, as clients of all service organizations, looked for effective service rather than ideological participation.

6. In other sources, Adizes (1971, chap. 8) discussed the problematic status of the director of a self-managed organization. He or she was under pressure both from the workers and the works councils and from the external political and economic markets. These pressures did not encourage many Yugoslav managers to take reasonable risks.[1]

In the first three decades after World War II, Yugoslavia enjoyed one of the world's highest rates of investment and economic growth. However, as Yugoslavia's GNP rose, workers became more interested in personal income than in either the socialist ideology of equality or the reinvestment of profits in the enterprise (Strauss, 1982). Thus, the Yugoslav practice of voting to turn profits into wage increases rather than into investment capital forced many self-managed firms to borrow large sums of money, until the loans were no longer cheap, and a national economic crisis was unavoidable. Adizes (1971) and Horvat (1971) remarked that, despite the ideology of self-management, Yugoslavia at that time was still a very centralized economy, and this fact was a barrier even to sincere efforts to decentralize decisions on wages, investments, and other managerial practices.

The deterioration of the self-management system and the whole political system of postwar Yugoslavia began after Tito's death in 1980, and reached its lowest point in 1992. However, the seeds of the destructive economic and social processes had been planted long before. Works councils in factories tended to favor short-term increases in wages at the expense of long-term capital investments in more productive equipment. Dissatisfaction with self-management and also with the diversion of profits to less-developed regions, played a large role in the secession of Croatia and Slovenia, both of which embarked on a program of economic privatization and complete repudiation of the socialist system. Socialist self-management remains in the reduced federation, but Serbia and Montenegro suffered from the loss of markets and sources of raw materials in the other republics, low work discipline and productivity, and difficulties competing in world markets.

THE UNITED STATES: COLLECTIVE BARGAINING

Contrary to the assertion in some quarters that in North America workers' participation was not a popular issue, contemporary historians, labor relations experts, and sociologists present evidence that participation always has been a desired goal in labor policy. This is embedded in the U.S. National Labor Relations Act (NLRA) and in similar Canadian acts, which were explicitly intended to encourage co-determination of conditions of employment through the practice of collective bargaining (Adams, 1992). Although that expectation has not been met, the NLRA has stimulated the expansion of collective bargaining, which took place during the 1930s and 1940s.

There is a strong argument that collective bargaining itself is a form of workers' participation. The reason is that workers force management, through union power, to consult, to share information, and to avoid unilateral measures that negatively affect them. Sanford Jacoby (1995) revealed that even management-sponsored company unions in the United States had strong features of industrial democracy. He made a distinction between representation plans [company unions] in the 1920s, and those adopted after the Wagner law in 1935. The adoption of representation plans in the 1920s was not merely for the purpose of impeding collective bargaining arrangements, but also to improve workplace efficiency, reduce labor turnover, control egregious foremen, get employees to identify with the firm, and strengthen the work ethics. Most of the representation plans after 1935 had one and only one purpose: to obstruct the formation of unions affiliated with the AFL or CIO. However, even then, liberal intellectuals, including Senator Wagner himself, had an understanding of collective bargaining as an integrative and cooperative institution, not an adversarial one, as is conventionally believed.

Whether collective bargaining is a form of workers' participation or not is a matter of definition. It does not contradict definitions of participation programs that are offered in this book (for example, Glew et al.'s definition, 1995, 26). However, we can examine the relevance of collective bargaining from a different point of view. Collective bargaining was the central institution of industrial relations in most countries where workers' participation programs were installed. In most cases, these programs complemented the industrial relations arrangements and did not challenge them or undermine them. In fact, they contributed to industrial peace that was the major goal of the collective bargaining system. Therefore, although collective bargaining was not a formal workers' participation program, it was not adverse to representative participation programs either.

THE FIRST GENERATION AS MIRRORED
IN THE IDE PROJECT

In the years 1975–1976 a research group from ten Western European countries, Yugoslavia, and Israel conducted an international study, entitled Industrial Democracy in Europe (IDE), on the impact of formal participation programs on actual participatory behavior and culture within enterprises (IDE, 1981). This integrative and international project reflects well the participation agenda of the major players in indirect representative programs of workers' participation, namely, the impact of a formal, legally prescribed system of participation in the actual distribution of power, involvement, and influence in organizations.

Data were obtained in the mid-1970s from 7,832 respondents employed in 154 manufacturing and service firms. The study revealed that countries with more formal participation of workers in decision-making and with more influence relative to management tended to be the countries with more rapid economic growth. Nations supporting higher interactive training and lower individualism among children appeared to have higher levels of formal worker participation and higher power distance in corporate culture.

In 1986 through 1987 another study replicated the earlier study (IDE, 1993). The sample for the replication, comprising key senior management and union respondents in 72 establishments, was evaluated to measure the influence of bargaining groups on industrial relations issues within participative structures. According to Bernhard Wilpert, the project coordinator, the main focus of the research was on the differential distribution of power and influence in organizations subject to different industrial democracy schemes. The core theoretical model postulated a relationship between formal rules for participation and the distribution of influence and participation in companies (measured by ranking key informants' influence and involvement in 16 types of decisions). Rosenstein found some patterns broadly similar across the countries under study: chronic unemployment in most of the countries, pressures for a reduction or stabilization of labor costs, and a call for greater flexibility in working conditions. Rosenstein said, "Generally speaking . . . industrial democracy was on the defensive" (Rosenstein, IDE, 1993, 68).

However, the impact of structural changes was rather uneven across countries. Drenth (IDE, 1993, chap. 3) presented comparisons among countries and over time with respect to formal participative systems, actual involvement practices, and the distribution of influence. Participation at higher levels of management was found to be influenced by the relevant board system, as was evidenced by the striking differences between the United Kingdom and Germany. Similarly, participation level F ("permanent representative bodies at the establishment level, no matter of what origin") included very dissimilar structures.

The replication study yielded evidence of substantial differences primarily in the formal participative structures, not so much in actual influence, which showed "remarkable stability over the ten years" (IDE, 1993, 96). Peccei (IDE, 1993, chap. 4.) analyzed contextual factors affecting patterns of influence distribution, such as organizational size, level of automation, perceived market dominance, and average unemployment rate. He concluded: "patterns of influence in organizations are not significantly conditioned by contextual factors" (IDE, 1993, 140) but rather by institutional norms mediated by historical conditions and by management strategy. Heller and Warner found that the common trend between the two studies from 1975 to 1976 and 1986 to 1987 was the attempt of companies to reduce the strength of labor during a recession. In fact, even where labor had been strong in the 1970s, it tended to lose ground between the two studies.

These conclusions fit well the argument of the changing generations in participation programs, which is discussed in Chapter 7.

NOTE

1. For a different view, by one who ran a self-managed firm, see Blum, 1970.

Chapter 7

Employee Involvement: The Second Generation

The second generation of participation programs covers the the most recent decades and could be called the era of employee involvement programs (EIP or EI), which is different from the previous era of workers' participation (WP) programs.[1] The assumptions, goals, strategies, structures, and operative modes of various workers' participation programs in the collective employment relations are quite different from those of the brave new world. Employee involvement, in this neo-capitalist framework, is an alternative and quite a different phenomenon—not participation for participation's sake, not participation as a vehicle to a harmonious work community, not participation as a power equalization mechanism, not participation as a strategy of industrial peace, and not participation as a means to industrial democracy.[2] But, on the contrary, this is participation in a novel sense, which relates to calculated, self-interested involvement.

Involvement partly provides a substitute for the above expectations and partly addresses different ones, namely, to improve the balance between inducements (rewards) and contributions (productivity), without the all-embracing vision of the work community. Thus, managers expect and design involvement structures and processes in order to enhance high performance and improve competitiveness. This includes upgrading skills, encouraging teamwork, developing commitment to quality, and enhancing work flexibility. Nowadays, participation by works councils and workers' representatives in managerial bodies is not greatly appreciated as a means to enhance productivity and competitiveness. In the current agenda, the old faith in human relations is replaced by new management theories. Thus, lean production, high performance, quality circles (QC), total quality management (TQM), just-in-time (JIT), reengineering, and other new guru theories enter the arena and join the new packages of employee involvement.[3] Again, pragmatism, rather than ideology; self-interest, rather than public interest; and productivity, rather than general work behavior, are the bon ton of the involvement issue.

EI programs began in the late 1970s and early 1980s with experiments with quality circles and quality of working life programs. Through the 1980s and 1990s, they proliferated, focusing on total quality management, continuous quality improvement (CQI), and other teamwork techniques (Kochan and Osterman, 1994; Ozaki, 1996). Lawler et al. (1995) assessed that the most commonly used EI practices in the 1980s were quality circles, task forces, quality improvement teams, and suggestion programs. Cotton (1993), in his comprehensive survey of the vast literature on employee involvement, was perhaps the most inclusive in his description of EI techniques. He included QWL programs, quality circles, gainsharing plans, representative participation, job enrichment, work teams, and employee ownership. However, he suggested a distinction between strong (self-directed work teams, gainsharing), intermediate (quality of working life, job enrichment, employee ownership), and weak employee involvement techniques (quality circles, representative participation). EI practices are often described as "parallel participation" structures because they work parallel to the formal organization. They are largely dependent on the regular organization for implementation, and do not radically alter the way in which the day-to-day work is performed.[4] Martin et al. (1995), Cotton et al. (1988), Griffin (1988), Marks et al. (1986), and Locke and Schweiger (1979) concluded that EI programs were tied to increased levels of satisfaction and organizational commitment. EI programs led to improved working conditions, provided greater opportunities for employee self-development, had a direct impact on productivity, and decreased absenteeism.

LEAN PRODUCTION AND TEAMWORK

Toward the end of the 1970s and the beginning of the 1980s, the economic situation in most of the developed countries worsened. Since then, intensifying competition in globalized markets has made enterprise survival dependent upon continuous improvements in productivity, in product and service quality, and in speed of delivery. These changes were caused and accelerated by the dizzying rise of new technologies: electronics, opto-electronics, robotics, informatics, biotechnology, and so forth. This new industrial and technological revolution and the intensifying global competition had a strong negative impact on employment levels in the developed countries. However, it also created strong demand for a new highly skilled, educated, and flexible labor force. Flexibility has become a key feature of high-performance work organizations.

In the new world of work, many firms perceived the older participation programs as luxurious, redundant, and irrelevant to the turbulent changes. Despite that attitude, many of the early ideas and experiments with socio-technical methods and autonomous work groups have come back into favor, with new names, as innovative solutions to the new requirements of flexibility and competitiveness (Braun and Senker, 1982; Walton, 1982; Emery, 1982). Indeed, they became the building blocks, in different configurations and terminology, of the involvement programs in the second generation.

Appelbaum and Batt (1994) identify "lean production" (LP) and "team production" as the two major practices that characterize the new high-performance enterprises.[5] The concept of lean production has been popularized by Womack et al. (1990), a group of researchers at the Massachusetts Institute of Technology. While there is a large and growing body of literature on the rise of lean production, Huxley and Robertson (1997) exposed the unpleasant aspect of LP, as viewed from the employees' point of view. They studied lean production techniques in the CAMI Automotive plant in Canada (a joint venture between General Motors and Suzuki, which opened in 1989). Under LP methods, they explored practices of recruitment and training of new workers for teamwork, the transfer of tasks from first-line supervisors to team leaders, job enrichment, job rotation, suggestion system, QCs, CQI, JIT delivery, and lean staffing (e.g., the elimination of relief workers and industrial engineers). The authors expected a more committed workforce and more harmonious labor-management relations. Instead, they found steady erosion of worker commitment to CAMI's values and goals. Actually, as the pace of work and workloads increased substantially, many workers were quoted as referring to CAMI as "just another car factory." The authors concluded that the essence of workers' dissatisfactions was a rigid adherence to a lean system dedicated to maximum output with minimal labor.

While team production has many features similar to lean production, its dependence on the active participation of front-line workers appears to contribute to more fundamental organizational change. Teamwork has many features in common with the autonomous work group of the socio-technical theories of the 1970s. The novelty of today's teamwork lies in the management-controlled teamwork, as opposed to autonomous group work, which was previously regarded as an instrument for enhancing quality of working life and industrial democracy. Nevertheless, the use of teams has expanded dramatically. For example, 82 percent of American companies with 100 or more employees reported that they use teams (Gordon, 1992). Sixty-eight percent of *Fortune* 1000 companies reported that they used self-managing work teams in 1993 compared to 28 percent in 1987 (Lawler et al., 1995).

DOWNSIZING AND OUTSOURCING

Downsizing of work organizations and outsourcing of a range of the firm's activities and capabilities are the results of many EI programs. One may trace this phenomenon of downsizing in the deindustrialization of the United States in the 1970s (Bluestone and Harrison, 1982), which led to the loss of blue-collar jobs and later to the loss of whitecollar jobs as well. This trend has been explained by several factors: technological breakthroughs, globalization of the economy, capital flight, and the shift from manufacturing to service industries (Eitzen and Zinn, 1989). However, unlike the layoffs in the past, it has involved restructuring of work organizations and designing of a new division of labor among the employees left behind.

Many companies have downsized. In a survey carried out every year by the American Management Association since 1987, an average of almost 50 percent of companies surveyed reduced their workforce. Greengard and Meissner (1993) reported that large U.S. firms announced nearly 600,000 layoffs. Work organizations expect downsizing to help them cut costs, reduce bureaucracy, help adapt to changes in the environment . . . and survive. However, downsizing has a negative impact on people who lose their jobs or are left behind, and results in lower morale and productivity, reduced loyalty, and burnout among managers (Cameron et al., 1988). Downsizing also has a negative impact on employee involvement, despite the claims of some consultants and personnel managers that organizations can heal the impaired morale and productivity by enhancing employee empowerment and team building. Employers, more often than perhaps is known, have to deal with the negative effects of downsizing. In contrast with the philosophy of regaining competitiveness through downsizing, a survey by the consulting firm Ernst and Young (*Success,* April 1996) showed that 80 percent of the top executives surveyed said that using teams and implementing compensation systems linked to performance, rather then using direct downsizing moves, made their companies more competitive. The results of another survey showed that fewer than half of all firms that have downsized since 1990 have reported short- or long-term operating profits, and 72 percent reported a decline in levels of worker morale (*The Economist,* October 26, 1996).

There is research evidence of a decrease in employee morale, loyalty, commitment, and innovation after layoff notification (Leana and Feldman, 1992). In a study of a unionized manufacturing facility, a part of an American multinational corporation, Martin et al. (1995) explored the relationships between an EI program and the effects of downsizing. The EI concept was introduced in 1986 by plant management as a means to manage costs and quality, and as an evolutionary step toward self-managing work teams. By the end of 1990, over 55 percent of the total nonmanagement work force were EI program members. Teams met for 1 hour each week and were led by team supervisors. Trained facilitators coordinated the overall program and provided support for the teams.

In the same year, the corporation pulled out a product line from the plant site and transferred it to an overseas manufacturing facility. This resulted in the permanent layoff of 210 skilled employees. The researchers found that EI membership did make a difference in worker responses to being discharged. Despite the fact that they faced permanent layoffs, EI members reported higher levels of organizational commitment and more favorable attitudes toward management than nonmembers faced with the same outcome. As compared to nonmembers, EI members were less severe in their assignment of blame to management and more severe in their assignment of blame to the union and to themselves. In other words, members may have felt that they "should have seen it coming" and been able to do something preemptively.

Outsourcing is the other side of the same phenomenon, and, as with downsizing, there is bound to be backlash. The soft management literature is full of accounts of disillusion and skepticism. For example, Scott Leibs reports in *Industry Week* (April 6, 1998) on this new reality that is taking hold in outsourcing. In a critical paper in the same month (*Industry Week,* April 20, 1998), John Mariotti attacks the tendency to view strategic outsourcing as a solution to every kind of problem. There are many genuine advantages to using third-party contractors. They may have special skills, knowledge, resources, and technology that the firm does not need to own. Outsourcing to a contractor who has complementary skills is even a smart idea. However, the story is different when the outsourcing deals with core activities of the firm. When the firm outsources its core competencies and capabilities, it may be giving away the whole business. Like any powerful medicine, if used incorrectly it can be deadly.

EMPLOYERS' ROLE

Since the 1980s, employers' concern has shifted from programs to improve working conditions for the sake of higher worker morale and industrial peace to EI programs to improve the quality of products, services, and productivity. However, since in many countries the trade unions and their allies are opposed to these programs, the employers' strategy has been to weaken this resistance everywhere.[6]

In the United Kingdom in the early 1980s, employers made every effort to regain unilateral control over work organization and reduce the influence of the trade unions and shop stewards. According to the 1990 Workplace Industrial Relations Survey (WIRS), they may have succeeded. Union-related constraints on their freedom to organize work were reported in only 16 percent of the establishments surveyed—and in only 10 percent in the private sector (Millward et al., 1992). In Germany, the metal industry employers' association was strongly opposed to the extension of works councils' co-determination rights to work organization issues (Jacobi and Hassel, 1996, 111–113). However, in larger firms, management generally seemed to believe that rationalization projects could not circumvent the works council. As a result, the practice of entering into an informal "modernization contract" between management, works councils, and employees was spread, particularly in the machine tool, automobile, and chemical industries (Mueller-Jentsch et al., 1992, 102–103).

Employers' reluctance to associate unions with EI programs was common in Australia, Japan, and the United States as well. Management in Japan generally regarded work organization as a matter of managerial prerogative. It usually informed unions of organizational changes, sometimes consulted them, but only rarely negotiated with them on such changes. In the United States, there were a number of high-performance companies with a strong union presence where management accepted a high degree of union-management cooperation in work organization (e.g., Xerox, Boeing Aerospace, AT&T, General Motors, Chrysler, Ford, and TWA). Nevertheless, a large majority of employers in the United States regarded unions as a hindrance to productivity and were unwilling to recognize them, let alone allow them to participate in decision-making on work organization.

In Italy, employers widely regarded collective bargaining as a means for reorganizing work and promoting direct participation. Similarly, Swedish employers generally accepted the principle of union-management cooperation in developing work organization. The French employers, since the decline of union power in the 1970s, unilaterally promoted various programs of employee involvement. Nevertheless, they attempted to make the 1982 act on "workers' right of expression" subject to union-management agreement. Thus, since the late 1980s, an increasing number of enterprises have started to negotiate collective agreements on issues related to work organization.

So, employers' policies toward EI programs were proactive and vigorous. As time passed, however, many of them have discovered the advantages of the unions' cooperation in these programs, but they are generally wary of rigid direct participation and excessive bureaucratic arrangements added by unions to these programs (Ozaki, 1996).

UNIONS' ROLE

In the new era of EI programs driven by employers' pursuit of higher competitiveness, unions were confronted with the challenge of defining new policies. Labor's initial response to EI programs tended either to reject completely or fully embrace the concept of EI.[7] In the intervening years, however, the labor movement has become considerably more sophisticated in its approaches to EI programs. The earlier ideological approach has been replaced by a more pragmatic approach that recognized the usefulness of EI programs to union goals.

In 1994, the European Foundation for the Improvement of Living and Working Conditions (EFILWC) carried out a survey of the positions of the European "social partners" (employers, unions, and so on) on direct participation in Europe (Regalia and Gill, 1995; 1996). According to the EFILWC survey, there were three main positions of unions:

1. *They are opposed to management-orchestrated participative programs.*
   Unions that adopted this position basically regarded such initiatives as a
   managerial device to exploit workers more efficiently and to seek to con-
   ceal the fundamental divergence of interests and inequality in power
   between employers and workers. Examples of unions that shared this
   view were Belgium's FGT and France's CGT-FO. German unions adopted
   similar positions as well throughout the 1980s. The position of the
   American AFL-CIO has been ambivalent until more recently. This attitude
   has support in some academic quarters. Some researchers still suspect
   that EI programs, at least in part, are being sponsored by management in
   an attempt to undermine unions and manipulate workers into working
   harder (Grenier, 1988). Parker (1985) expressed these strategic fears of
   labor that "Toyotism" is not an alternative to 'Taylorism," but rather a
   solution to the classic problem of the resistance of the workers to production rationalization."[8]

2. *Management-initiated EI programs are an opportunity.* According to this
   approach, EI programs can improve the quality of work and increase
   workers' influence at shop floor level, while enhancing the competitiveness of the company. Unions that adopt this position seek to play an
   active part in organizational reform through representative forms of participation, including collective bargaining. Scandinavian and Italian
   unions generally fall into this category. France's CFDT, the sponsor of the
   1982 Act on "worker's right of expression," has been in favor of
   employee participation for more than two decades. Germany's IG Metall
   and DGB adopted this position in the 1990s (Jacobi and Hassel, 1996). In
   1994 the AFL-CIO publicly endorsed labor-management partnerships for
   purposes of introducing new models of work organization and employee
   participation (Kochan and Osterman, 1994, 165–166). In the United
   Kingdom, where unions have been almost uniformly hostile to new
   forms of work organization, the Trades Union Congress has increasingly
   recognized the need for more flexible production systems.

3. *Participation falls within the managerial domain.* According to this position, unions should not seek to influence EI initiatives. This is typically
   the position taken by most Japanese unions. Work organization is an area
   of enterprise management in which union involvement is indeed
   markedly weaker in Japan than in many other industrialized countries. As
   a matter of fact, many shop floor union representatives in Japan are
   group leaders or team leaders, who otherwise participate in decisions
   concerning work organization.

The various reactions of labor unions to EI programs well reflect the disarray and confusion in organized labor movements. They reveal the lack of coherent labor theory and strategy in the new post-modern second generation, where identities of allies and foes, and concepts of good and evil are blurred and constantly changing. The well-recognized and relatively small group of players in the participation game are replaced by many and different players. Also, the central arena of participation programs moved to a different continent—to North America.

NOTES

1. The literature on EI is expansive. See, for example, Lawler et al., 1992, 1995; Marchington et al., 1992; McCaffrey et al., 1995.

2. The researchers of the Industrial Democracy in Europe (IDE), with its emphasis on industrial democracy and power sharing are aware of the changes during this decade (p. 148): "Over the ten years [1977–1987], labour tended to lose ground in organizations where it had been strong in the seventies. Management strategy of reducing the strength of labour . . . was facilitated in places where unemployment was high. Where unemployment was not high and labour was not particularly strong in the 1977 research, the influence of workers did not change very much. In these circumstances it is quite likely that management initiated quasi-participative human resources measures, like briefing groups and various employee involvement programs, including quality circles . . ." (IDE, Research Group, 1993).

3. Baillie (1995) highlighted the adoption of EI practices as streaming after guru theories in management. By reference to total quality management, human resource management, and employee involvement, he described the amusing case where it was almost impossible to attend a conference or read a specialist journal over the last decade without someone trying to convince you that these practices were critical to your organization's performance. In the late 1980s and into the 1990s, these topics were being preached with a gospel-like fervency.

4. Hyman and Mason (1996) drew the difference between employee involvement and workers' participation, EI are practices that emanate from management and purport to provide employees with the opportunity to influence decision-making on matters that affect them. Employee participation, on the other hand, refers to initiatives, which promote the collective rights of employees to be represented in organizational decision-making, including collective bargaining. The European countries exhibit this approach with works councils, employee representation on boards, and financial participation.

5.   Various surveys of work practices showed that many firms have implemented at least a few innovative work practices, but that these practices typically cover a small fraction of a firm's workforce and that no particular practices predominate. See Osterman (1994). His survey had a response rate of 66 percent and was limited to establishments with 50 or more employees (which employ more than half of all workers). An establishment could be a headquarters or a division of a company. Practices examined were teams, job rotation, total quality management, and quality circles.

6.   In some cases, employers promoted EI programs to weaken the trade unions. Grenier and Hogler (1991) showed how hostile management used an employee involvement program to block attempts to unionize during the union organizing campaign.

7.   The U.S. Department of Labor publication *Labor-Management Cooperation: Perspectives from the Labor Movement* (1984) provides an example of these early, relatively simplistic responses.

8.   Hodson et al. (1992) found, in a sample of 371 employees in an American company, that increased worker autonomy and participation led to a similar increase in worker solidarity, and that increased worker autonomy did not decrease solidarity and had only a limited effect on a sense of injustice at the workplace. Thus, the fear that autonomy will increase worker consent and erode a critical stance toward management was not supported.

Chapter 8

Major Players of Employee Involvement

In the first generation of participation programs, the dominant players were European countries and organizations. Both indirect and direct forms of participation were pioneered and experienced in European enterprises and research institutions. In the second generation of employee involvement programs, the dominant player was the United States, with influence of the Japanese work organization. Europe and other countries in this period adopted innovations in the field rather than initiating them.

THE UNITED STATES: REDISCOVERING PRAGMATISM

Since the 1980s, there has been a substantial expansion in the number and variety of employee participation programs and workplace committees in both establishments governed by collective-bargaining agreements and those without union representation. These arrangements take a wide variety of forms such as quality circles, employee-participation teams, total quality management teams, safety and health committees, gain-sharing plans, joint labor-management training programs, information-sharing forums, joint task forces for a variety of problems, employee-ownership programs, and worker representation on corporate boards of directors.

This change has been driven in part by international and domestic competition, technology, and workforce developments. However, the external forces have been accompanied by a growing recognition that achieving a high-performance economy requires changing traditional methods. The required changes were of labor-management relations and the organization of work in ways that more fully develop and utilize the skills, knowledge, and motivation of the workforce and that share the gains produced.

Given the fact that there was a general lack of interest in participation programs in the United States prior to the 1980s, evidence of a remarkable change was reflected in the Commission on the Future of Worker-Management Relations in 1993. This was comparable in importance, perhaps, to the task force on Work in America in the 1970s. The commission was announced by Secretary of Labor Robert Reich and Secretary of Commerce Ronald Brown on March 24, 1993, and was chaired by John Dunlop. Its first question to report was: "What (if any) new methods or institutions should be encouraged, or required, to enhance work-place productivity through labor-management cooperation and employee participation"?

On June 2, 1994, the Secretaries of Labor and Commerce released the Fact-Finding Report of the Commission and an Executive Summary. The first item in the mission statement that the committee issued is striking: "Expand coverage of employee participation and labor-management partnerships to more workers and more workplaces and to a broader array of decisions." The trigger for the Dunlop Commission was two cases of violating the labor law of the National Labor Relations Board (NLRB). The first was the case of Electromation, an Indiana electronics company. The company had set up joint employee-management committees. Shortly after the committees were established, the Teamsters union attempted to organize the plant and lodged an NLRB complaint about the committees. In a major ruling, including the failure of an appeal to the Seventh Circuit, the NLRB held that the committees violated section 8(a)(2). They were illegal because the company helped to form the committees and the committees represented employees in dealings with the employer over terms and conditions of employment. Yet Electromation did not make it clear as to precisely when employers could or could not set up committees, teams, and other EI programs.

These questions were clarified in the DuPont case. DuPont established joint labor-management committees at one of its unionized plants, and the NLRB held the committees to be unlawful. Attached to the DuPont decision were guidelines telling employers how to set up EI programs that would comply with the National Labor Relations Act. Briefly, the NLRB held that an EI program might be lawful (1) if it dealt exclusively with management functions, such as an entirely self-managing team; (2) if the EI program were a rotating group or an assembly of all employees that had no leaders or spokespersons; (3) if the EI program involved sharing information or "brainstorming" with employees without making proposals; and (4) if the EI program were a one-way body, such as a suggestion box.

The AFL-CIO supported these rulings, since for them nonunion EI programs were an impediment to union organizing and could not possibly meet the full range of employee needs. The employer community, however, was not happy with the decisions and has sought legislation to counter them. One such bill would allow employers to set up EI programs. The "Teamwork for Employees and Management Act" (TEMA) permits EI programs to deal with "matters of mutual interest (including issues of quality, productivity, and efficiency)" as long as these EI programs do not negotiate or modify an existing labor contract. The Clinton administration found itself in a difficult position in the debate over EI programs in 1993, and the Dunlop Commission was a way to resolve these issues.

Whatever the detailed occurrence, it marked a shift in the American attitude toward participation. In "The Worker Representation and Participation Survey," a national survey of American employees conducted by Princeton Survey Research Associates in the fall of 1994, which was cited by the committee, we get a picture of employee involvement in the United States today. This study is a detailed and in-depth analysis of workplace practices and of the attitudes and views of workers on workplace issues.[1] It presents the views of a representative sample of over 2,400 employees in privately owned firms with greater than 25 workers. It identifies workers and supervisors, current union members, prior members, and nonmembers, as well as the diverse demographic groups that make up the American workforce.

The major findings of the survey, relating to employee involvement, are briefly summarized as follows: American workers want more involvement and greater say in their jobs. They would like this involvement to take the form of joint committees with management and would prefer to elect members of those committees rather than have managers select them. They prefer cooperative committees to potentially adversarial organized relationships.

One-third of the employees reported being involved with self-directed work teams, total quality management, quality circles, or other forms of employee involvement programs, and over half reported that such programs exist at their firms. Most employees wanted more influence or decision-making power in their job, and believed this would improve company productivity as well as their working lives, and almost two-thirds of employees said they wanted more influence.

The debate in the United States around the commission reflects basic dilemmas in the American industrial relations. Since the 1970s, the industrial relations system in the United States has been experiencing a huge contraction in private sector unionism (currently only 11 percent—half the rate of 25 years ago) and rapid expansion of team-based production and other forms of employee participation in the workplace. Osterman (1994) showed that EI programs have made a significant expansion in American companies. EI programs initially took hold in the nonunion sector and are now spreading to unionized firms as well. These new programs, however, run counter to that of the traditional adversarial model of collective bargaining.

Some argued that the unions' position is due to coercion by employers, who pressure and threaten employees not to join unions, and undoubtedly such employer behavior occurs during union organizing campaigns. It is also likely, however, that they fail to deal with the new work relations' patterns. Indeed, in a provocative study, Farber (1990) found that the decline in demand for union representation in the United States could be accounted for almost entirely by an increase in nonunion employees' job satisfaction.

Pivec and Robbins (1996) elaborated on the controversial employee involvement in the United States by emphasizing that times change. Employees today are not the laborers of the early twentieth century, whose work consisted of narrow, repetitive tasks. Technological advances and the development of a globally competitive marketplace have compelled changes in industrial relations. Employees are increasingly involved in solving problems and making decisions that were once the province of management. Committees and other cooperative programs often address workplace issues such as safety, efficiency, and quality.

Delaney (1996) put the Dunlop Commission in perspective. He argued that the central question is whether the proposed solutions in the commission's recommendations facilitate the achievement of sustainable economic competitive advantage and the promotion of civil society. One proposal that may balance both economic and social objectives is the encouragement of work systems based on employee participation in decision-making. Inherent in the idea of giving employees a voice is the notion that their desire to participate is coupled with their will to work harder and smarter in return for participation opportunities. Participation also can stimulate the development of civil society because it encourages individuals to develop and practice habits that are critical to self-sufficiency, self-rule, and the development of individual responsibility (recall Pateman, 1970). However, Delaney argued that participation cannot be mandated and can occur where both the employer and employees desire it.

In a reply to Delaney, Coxson (1996), in an attack on "groups of union officials, joined by a small vocal minority of labor law professors, who have stubbornly challenged needed legislative reforms to the National Labor Relations Act to encourage workplace cooperation," called him to draw the conclusions from his own analysis in favor of a significant reform in the legislation of the NLRB. He cited Delaney himself on the mismatch between yesterday's labor laws and today's workplace realities, and complained that the Clinton administration gave in to a small powerful cadre of union leaders whose political support was needed before the 1996 presidential election. Since the publication of the Dunlop report, no significant change in legislation has occurred, and there is still a huge gap between a reality of growing experience with EI and the U.S. labor law.[2]

North American labor-management tradition is not a lack of participation aspirations and practices. This tradition is practical and related to ideals of communalism and individualism rather than political ideals of industrial democracy as in Europe. The revival of the participation agenda in the United States in the 1990s is a fascinating litmus test for both the social undercurrents in American society and the changing faces of participation in work organizations.

THE EUROPEAN UNION: BRIDGING
THE GENERATION GAP

The European Union (EU) is not homogeneous on the issue of participation programs. Lines of differences divide the United Kingdom from continental Europe, the Scandinavian block from the rest of Europe, northern countries from southern countries, East Europe from West Europe, and so forth. However, participation and involvement in the last decades in European countries are not only social and economic issues but also attempts to develop a European way of life and all-embracing strategy. The programs, the debates, and the research are therefore rooted in a long tradition of participation, in some cases even pioneering experience, on which the Europeans want to build. The participation issue in Europe in the last decades is influenced by two major factors: the unification process and the policies of welfarism of the postwar era.

In his study of employee participation in EU countries, Herman Knudsen (1995) documented the change during the decades after World War II, where increased and formalized employee participation in workplace decision-making reached an apex in the 1960s. There then followed a long period of inactivity, if not retreat, even in Germany, where extensive workers' participation rights, anchored in national law, had been enacted. In the last decade, after the adoption of the Maastricht accords, efforts to enact an EU-wide "social charter" were consistently blocked by Britain's Conservative government, which strongly resisted the concept of formal worker participation in enterprise decision-making.[3] A dramatic change took place in Britain on May 1, 1997, with the election of a Labor government. One of the first actions taken by Prime Minister Tony Blair was to notify the EU that Britain would accede to the "social charter" and establish the forms of worker participation provided in it, thereby ending the British hold-out on such issues as elected works councils and their right to participate in enterprise decision-making.

Knudsen studied four countries in detail: Germany, Britain, Spain, and Denmark. Of these four, the German model has had the strongest influence on EU-wide developments, in spite of strong national historical differences. Yet these different approaches occurred within a common European framework, especially during the period since the creation of a "common market" in the Treaty of Rome in 1958. He asserted that national institutions and their historical legacies will continue to distinguish trade unions and works councils in Germany (with its strong tradition of formal and legal regulation) from those of Denmark (characterized by a long informal, cooperative inheritance) and Spain (marked by the struggle of the workers against the Franco regime). However, there will be growing convergence in the pattern of workplace governance.

As noted, the United Kingdom is a special case in its resistance to the old types of workers' participation programs. However, in EI programs the picture is different. Evidence from two major sources, the workplace industrial relations survey (WIRS) and employers' manpower and skills practices survey (EMSPS) in 1990, supported the claim that the proportion of organizations with EI programs is higher than is perhaps commonly assumed. In another publication, Wood and Menezes (1998) explored practices identified with high commitment management (HCM), which is their term for high-performance organizations. They found 23 common practices of HCM related to EI.[4]

The EI efforts on a European level are quite extensive. The institutionalization of European works councils was discussed in Chapter 2. Another initiative is a Green Paper ("Partnership for a new organization of work") of the European Commission, which on April 16, 1997, invited the social partners, public authorities, and other interested bodies to provide inputs to a framework designed to encourage European firms to render work organization more flexible, while at the same time improving security for workers. The Green Paper emphasized the importance of the development of an integrated approach in relation to employment and competitiveness, taxation and social protection issues, the information society, worker involvement, macro-economic and structural policies, and education and training.[5]

The most important research on the state of the European participation programs today is the "Employee Direct Participation in Organizational Change" (EPOC) project—a major investigation of the nature and role of direct participation, which was launched by the European Foundation for the Improvement of Living and Working Conditions in 1992. Activities so far have included work on the concept of direct participation; a study of the attitudes of the social partners throughout Europe; an appraisal of available research in the United States, Japan, and the European Union; round tables and conferences of social partners and government representatives, and a representative postal survey of workplaces in EU countries (*Euroline,* November 1998).

Ten countries were involved: Denmark, France, Germany, Ireland, Italy, Netherlands, Portugal, Spain, Sweden, and the United Kingdom. Respondents were workplace managers. The survey covered the views of management in nearly 6,000 establishments. Managers responding to the EPOC survey believed that direct participation in organizational change works. Each of the forms of direct participation was viewed as having positive effects on a range of performance indicators, such as quality, output, costs, and through-put times, on absenteeism and sickness, and on reductions in the number of employees and managers. For example, 56 percent of managers saw a significant cost reduction as a result of group-work, while 94 percent saw quality improvements. Practicing one form of direct participation intensively seems to work

better than practicing several forms to a limited extent. Direct participation measures, such as suggestion schemes, "speak-up schemes," and
project groups, are as important for good economic performance and
for reductions in labor costs as group-work. The greater the responsibility given to employees, the better and more sustainable are the economic results.

The scope of much of the direct participation, which is practiced
by the European enterprise, was rather limited. In the case of Japan,
group-work was found to be practiced by more than 90 percent of
large companies in industry and more than 80 percent in services. A
comparison of the prevalence of integrated forms of group-work
show the United States at 41 percent (1994) and Europe at 16 percent
(1996). Thus the coverage in the United States is two and a half times
higher than the European average. Sweden has the highest rate in
Europe, with 31 percent of all establishments where more than 50
percent of the workers are working in teams. Only a very small proportion (around 2 percent) of organizations in the 10 EU member
countries were pursuing the "Scandinavian" model, which is defined,
for the present purposes, as high-intensity group-work, plus a quali-
fied workforce, plus high-intensity training. This is particularly surprising given that their respective sponsors judged the "Scandinavian"
model to be more successful than the so-called "Toyota" equivalent
(low-intensity group-work, plus medium or low employee skills, plus
low-intensity training). In most countries, the consultative forms were
regarded as more important than delegation. Indeed, many managers
who practiced group-work did not necessarily regard it as the most
important form.

A number of ingredients for success were identified. One is qualifi-
cation and training: The better the employee qualifications and vocational training, the more likely that direct participation will be
successful in achieving its various benefits. Similarly, direct participation
was more likely to be successful if employees and managers were
trained for such participation. Training in social skills, and not just vocational training, was very important for managers as well as for
employees. A second success ingredient was the involvement of
employee representatives in the introduction of direct participation.

Another European vehicle for transmission of information and
reporting experience on participation until 1997 was the *P+ European
Participation Monitor*—a publication of the European Foundation for
the Improvement of Living and Working Conditions. The purpose of

this publication was to promote participation in many ways in the EU member states. In its 13 issues from 1991 to 1997, one can form a picture of the participation agenda among the EU member states. The material is a mix of detailed case studies in various European companies, conference proceedings, policy discussions, and some academic research studies. There were several themes in the P+ issues: participation in management, works councils, socio-technical systems (STS), autonomous groups, teamwork, TQM, CQI, employee involvement, and economic participation. I performed agenda setting analysis on these themes, and I found it is possible to reduce this set of articles into three topics:

1. *Workers' participation (WP)*—includes industrial democracy projects, participation in management, works councils (also the European Unions), and integrative collective bargaining
2. *Employee involvement (EI)*—includes information sharing, empowerment programs, QC, ESOP, and other schemes of economic participation
3. *Work reform (WR)*—includes STS, autonomous work groups, teamwork, TQM, CQI, and so on.

Figure 8.1 is an attempt to portray the European agenda on participation in the 1990s as reflected in P+. The *x*-axis is the year of publication. The *y*-axis represents the saliency of the various issues in P+, namely, WP, EI, and WR.

The most frequently used type of workers' participation and works councils is the older type of program. The less frequently used type is the EI programs, and the WR type is covered almost every year between 1991 and 1997.

The European second generation of participation programs reflects the efforts of EU member states, labor organizations, and companies to adapt to the new economic, technological, and social challenges in Europe and outside and at the same time to preserve the core European way of industrial democracy.

ISRAEL: BETWEEN TWO GENERATIONS

The story of the Israeli experience with participation programs is a story of decline. The development of workers' participation and employee involvement in Israel since the 1960s was influenced by the general characteristics of the Israeli system of industrial relations. This

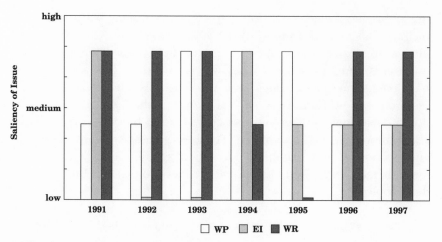

FIGURE 8.1. *Trends in participation agenda in Europe as reflected in P+.*

system was highly unionized and centralized in its collective bargaining practices as well as having strong shop committees at the local level. The Israeli industry at that time was organized in three main sectors: the private sector; the public sector, which included important industries such as aircraft, military equipment, and petro-chemicals; and what was termed the "labor economy," that is, enterprises belonging to the General Federation of Labor (Histadrut). Some idea of the size of this last sector can be gained from the fact that in 1984 it accounted for 21 percent of the industrial labor force in Israel, 26 percent of the country's industrial export (excluding diamonds), and 35 percent of industrial investments.[6] Formal indirect representative participation of workers in management existed only in the Histadrut's enterprises.

The position of the Histadrut in the participation and /or involvement issue was always complicated. Unlike the typical federation of trade unions, the Histadrut had aspired, since its establishment in 1920, to be a voluntary, all-embracing organization of all wage and salary earners. In attempting to create a sort of "Workers' Society," the Histadrut encompasses labor unions, business organizations, and services such as health care, pension funds, vocational training, sports, and cultural institutions. By acting as entrepreneur and owner of the means of production, the Histadrut's goal was to create a nonexploitative work organization in which labor and capital are not alienated from each other.

However, the contradiction between the Histadrut's dual role as both an employer and workers' organization has always been difficult to reconcile. Since the mid-1960s, considerable differentiation within the growing Histadrut membership, in living standards and social background of Histadrut members, and the increased size and bureaucratization of the labor economy have given rise to a growing sense of unease in its business enterprises. Managers, who have been encouraged to run efficient and profitable enterprises, have tended to adopt capitalistic notions of industrial leadership. Most workers, on the other hand, have seen themselves first and foremost as trade unionists and have sought to strengthen the position of their shop-floor committees and local union officials, rather than any commitment to the broader socialist values of the Histadrut. In the absence of such commitment, alienation between workers, managers, and Histadrut officials was inevitable. The proposed remedies for this alienation were workers' participation and industrial democracy.

Direct participation programs in Israel were developed in three areas: quality of working life, quality circles, and quality management. The QWL programs were centered in the work of the Socio Technical Force (STF) team of the Kibbutzim Industries Association. This group consisted of social scientists and industrial engineers specializing in organizational development (OD). Their participatory strategy was based on STS principles and autonomous work groups (Golomb, 1981). The group was influenced by ideas and concepts of the quality of working life movement and was active mainly in the kibbutzim themselves or in regional industrial enterprises belonging to and managed by the kibbutzim, but employing non-kibbutz-member workers.

Later on, the STF extended its activities to consultancy and management training in QWL-STS strategies and techniques and in helping to establish Greenfield industrial sites. According to a report by the Kibbutzim Industries Association, the number of projects carried out in industrial enterprises and the demand for the STF's services were increasing steadily every year during the 1980s. However, the penetration of QWL-STS applications to other sectors was slow (exceptionally important cases were a project of job redesign in the pharmaceutical company Teva, and several other companies).[7]

On the other hand, there was rapid growth of quality circles in several big companies, both in the public sector and in the labor economy. In 1987 there were an estimated 250 quality circles in the aircraft industry, the chemical industry, the military industry, several electronics companies, and other companies from all sectors.[8] Quality management techniques have been implemented in Israel since the 1980s, either under the various titles of TQM, or the various versions of ISO.

I applied agenda setting to the issue of participation programs in Israel, in order to see what happened in the three areas (workers' participation, employee involvement, and direct participation). I retrieved from the Index to Hebrew Periodicals (IHP) at Haifa University all the published items in the field between 1977 and 1997. I found 275 usable items in 26 periodicals, according to eight issues: workers' participation, employee involvement, industrial democracy, STS and autonomous groups, QWL, QC, economic participation, and quality management. I then combined the eight issues into three:

1. W: Workers' participation, economic participation[9] and industrial democracy
2. EI: Employee involvement in QC and QWL
3. WR: Work reform in STS and TQM

Finally, in Figure 8.2 charted the time series of the three areas (with moving averages smoothing).

As we can see in Figure 8.2, in the past two decades the representative workers' participation issue declined dramatically from an issue that attracted most of the public and professional interest in the 1970s and then almost disappeared in the 1990s. In the following sections, I elaborate on this amazing (some would say sad) decline.

As in other countries, the popularity of EI issues soared in the 1980s and declined in the early 1990s. However, we also see a resurgence of the EI issue in the second half of the 1990s. I can only guess that since in Israel EI packages are more heterogeneous than WP's or WR's packages, people refer to the concepts in this family in a looser sense.

The WR trend has a similar pattern as in other countries: becoming "in" during the late 1980s, and then losing momentum and prevalence toward the second half of the 1990s. So, the general patterns of the participation agenda in Israel reflect the changes both in the real economic and organizational world and in the image of this world in the published media. However, WP's trend, which is connected to the Histadrut, deserves further elaboration.

PARTICIPATION IN THE HISTADRUT: A BATTLE
FOR THE SOULS OF ALIENATED WORKERS

In this section I discuss two programs in a unionized setting in Israel in the 1970s and 1980s that illustrate the shift from a politico-ideolog-

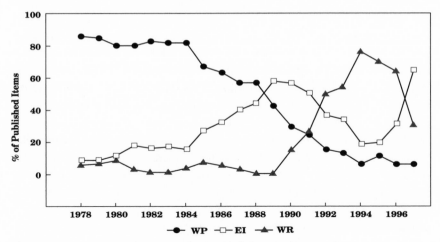

FIGURE 8.2. *Participation agenda in Israel (moving averages).*

ical workers' participation to managerial-centered employee involvement.

In the 1970s the core element in the participation programs of the Histadrut was the Joint Management Committees (JMCs). These bodies were composed of workers' and management's representatives, usually up to four members on each side plus the enterprise's CEO as a chairman, and were empowered, inter alia, to discuss and propose policy guidelines on a wide range of personnel issues. According to one report, there were 105 Joint Management Committees in 1984.[10] The JMCs have played a positive role in reducing some of the heat and animosity in labor relations in many Histadrut enterprises.[11] However, they have been unable to establish a fully participatory system, because to do so would have been to trespass on the negotiating functions of the existing shop-floor committees. Thus, the JMCs, while responding to important political and ideological objectives of the Histadrut, have been unable to convince the mass of ordinary workers of their utility. See Figure 8.3.

In the 1980s the political and economic situations changed. The defeat of the Labor Party in the general election of 1977 accelerated the search for new ways to convince workers and voters of the unique nature of the labor sector. A shift occurred also in the balance of power, strengthening the business sector of the Histadrut at the expense of its political barons. The need to compete effectively in local and global markets and the termination of the taken-for-granted governmental support forced the Histadrut to pay greater attention to its business leaders. The latter did not care much for the Histadrut's socialist image. Instead, they strove for productivity, competitiveness, and profitability. They also were exposed to and attracted by a wide range of new managerial techniques, prevailing in the business enterprises of their local and international competitors. Among these new techniques were QC, QWL, teamwork, autonomous work group, and the like. Fortunately, some of these techniques were not far from the vocabulary of the older participation programs, but now everyone referred to them as Employees Involvement (EI) with emphasis on cooperation and collaboration rather than workers' control, or industrial democracy, with political and ideological class struggle connotations.

The main effort in setting up EI in the Histadrut was concentrated in its industrial company Koor, which at that time was the largest industrial conglomerate in Israel. The initiative, this time, was taken by Koor management and was very different from that of the JMCs. Both were top-down attempts to introduce change. However, as noted before, the aims of the Histadrut were to install in its enterprises industrial democracy and power-sharing arrangements. Koor, on the other hand, attempted to develop a strategy of employee involvement that would enhance better utilization of human resources.[12] This idea was sup-

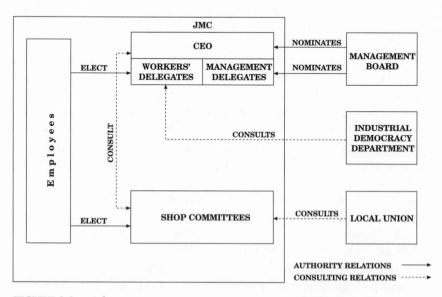

FIGURE 8.3. *Schematic joining management program in the histadrut.*

posed to be implemented in a "Social Program" that would (a) maintain workers' participation in information (that is, the continuation of the JMCs); (b) introduce quality circles to develop human resources (mainly new management cadres) but also train the entire labor force in new skills and work methods; and (c) promote quality of working life programs and devise social services with more attention to the needs and priorities of the work community.[13]

The setup of the Social Program included the following guidelines: In every enterprise, the program, directed by a steering committee, consisted of the CEO, personnel manager, and workers' representative. The steering committee establishes subcommittees and prepares an annual work plan with appropriate budgeting. The plan is submitted to Koor's center for approval. The steering committee meets every 3 months to monitor the program and guide the activists.

The CEO is expected to involve workers in information, production, and work processes. He or she is personally responsible for presenting annual work schedules, performance reports, and correction measures in case of failure. The CEO and the steering committee also have to initiate communication workshops at all levels, and arrange for a series of periodic meetings: departmental meetings every 2 weeks; monthly meetings between the top management team and rank-and-file employees, and meetings between the CEO and groups of workers at least three times a year.

Other responsibilities of the steering committee include training workers' representatives in managerial skills; training in preparation of professional presentations for the joint management and employees' meetings; continuation of the JMCs in those enterprises in which they were still active; setting up teams of workers, engineers, and managers to improve and humanize work methods and processes; upgrading the entire labor force in the enterprise by general education classes and training in new work methods and quality assurance; better human resource management, which uses career planning and rotations at work and special provisions for shift workers and working mothers. Other target areas of expected activities were investment in the aesthetic appearance of the enterprise and the work stations and the means to communicate with the families and the community by publishing a newsletter and other contacts and projects.

The Social Program was introduced in several dozen Koor enterprises. As expected, it involved a fairly large number of rank-and-file workers in a variety of activities: vocational training, EAP programs, running subsidized shops, entertainment and leisure, educational classes for workers and their children, social clubs, and so on.[14] In a study that was conducted in five enterprises, it was found that the figures, though technically impossible to compare with the JMCs in the 1979 study, paint a rather more positive picture, especially since they reflect rank-and-file attitudes.[15] Between 1984 and 1988 the program had accumulated momentum and diversified experience. In the "average" enterprise with SP, there were quality circles, communication activities, and vocational training courses.

In the late 1980s the business situation of Koor worsened. Its competitiveness and profitability declined dangerously to the point of receivership. Its creditors in Israel and abroad, including the government (one of Koor's major creditors) forced Koor to initiate a major recovery program. Mass redundancies, the shutdown of dozens of unprofitable plants, and painfully drastic organizational, technological, and business restructuring have made Koor leaner and more profitable. Also in this recovery process, EI has been restructured: Instead of an integrated program for all of Koor's enterprises, local management-driven initiatives, with all the ingredients of similar high-performance corporations in other countries, were encouraged.[16] Israeli financial groups and U.S. firms completed the privatization process of Koor by total takeover.

The privatization of Koor was only one endeavor, albeit the most dramatic one, among many other privatization moves to put an end to the Histadrut ownership of its business organizations. This strategic move has nearly been completed, especially since the political and ideological upheaval in the Histadrut's elections of 1994, when a new coalition of both leftist and rightist, even religious ultra-orthodox groups took over and changed even the name of the Histadrut to "New Histadrut."

NOTES

1. Where questions overlap, the Worker Representation and Participation Survey findings are consistent with those of earlier surveys, such as the 1976 Quality of Employment Survey sponsored by the U.S. Department of Labor conducted by the University of Michigan; the Penn and Shoen survey conducted by the LPA; the Harris Poll conducted for the AFL-CIO; Industrial Relations Counselors, Inc., Report on the IRC Survey of Employee Involvement, August 1994, among others.

2. In a personal communication with the author on March 1998, Tom Kochan was sorry to report that the Dunlop report had no impact on either

policy, or as far as anyone can tell, on practice (with the exception of some expanded use of Alternative Dispute Resolution in discrimination cases).

3.   A typical piece that demonstrates the British attitude of the time is by Graham Hallett in *Management Today,* June 1990, 31–32. He surveyed the issue of employee involvement as being raised again and again at EC level. The Government and the CBI opposed any legislation on employee representation. Britain was the only state with no legal provisions on employee representation.

4.   Within WIRS90 there are questions on the following practices: quality circles/problem-solving groups, appraisal, merit pay, profit-sharing, welfare facilities or fringe benefits, information disclosure, team briefing, top management briefing, suggestion schemes, and attitude surveys; while EMSPS contains information on the following practices: internal recruitment, multiskilling, social skills as a selection criterion, teamwork skills as a selection criterion, and training needs analysis.

5.   European initiatives in the field are growing all the time. For example, in November 1997, a group of experts on "European systems of worker involvement," known as the Davignon group, set out recommendations for the information, consultation, and board-level participation of employees in the European company. The Union of Industrial and Employers' Confederations of Europe (UNICE) responded to this report in a positive way. However, UNICE stressed that such an instrument must remain flexible voluntarily, since most member states do not provide for worker participation in corporate bodies.

6.   Annual Report of Hevrat Ovdim. 1984. 25–29 (In Hebrew).

7.   Annual Report of the Kibbutzim Industries Association. October 1985 (In Hebrew). Golomb, N. (1981). "Socio-technical Strategy for Improving the Effectiveness and the QWL of Three Kibbutz Plants and One Governmental Institute." Paper Presented at the International Conference on the QWL and the 80's. August 30–September 3, Toronto, Canada. Shelhav, M., and Golomb, N. (1986). "Socio-technical Improvements in Plants of the Kibbutz's Industry." Paper Presented at the International Conference on QWL and the Kibbutz, June 26–28, Israel. (In Hebrew). Report of the Israeli IIRA Task Force on "Quality of Working Life in Israel." (In Hebrew). Tel-Aviv. 25–26.

8.   Hashavya, A. (1985). "Proper Management from the Bottom." Be'Koor Ekhad. July, 15–17. (In Hebrew). The Israeli IRRA task force, op cit., and 46–47. Elizur D. (1987). "Quality Circles and Quality of Work Life." Paper Presented at the Second European Regional Congress of Industrial Relations, Herzelia, Israel.

9.   In some countries, economic participation in the forms of gain sharing or profit sharing is attached to EI packages. In Israel, however, the few published items in this category are in the context of representative indirect workers' participation programs.

10. Hevrat Ovdim, op. cit., 44.

11. See Bar-Haim, A. (1979). "Workers' Participation in the Management of Industrial and Craft Plants." Work and Welfare Research Institute. The Hebrew University of Jerusalem (In Hebrew).

12. At that time the term was "participative management" as opposed to "workers' participation.".

13. Kotzer, R. (1984). The Social Program of Koor. In: Yad-Tabenkin, Haifa University and the Histadrut Working Papers Series, No. 44, 25–34 (Hebrew).

14. Such services were common in many Israeli companies. See: Bargal, D., and Shamir, B. (1980). "Welfare Services in Workplaces: Characteristics and Roles." Work and Welfare Research Institute. The Hebrew University of Jerusalem (Hebrew); The Israeli IRRA task force, op cit., 74–75.

15. See Bar-Haim, A., Bar-Yosef , R., and Hochman, R. (1985). "The Social Program in Koor: An Evaluation Study in Five Plants." Work and Welfare Research Institute. The Hebrew University of Jerusalem (Hebrew).

16. On the characteristics of lean and high- performance organizations, see a special issue of the *Applied Psychology: An International Review,* 1996, 45, 2, 97–152.

Part III

A General Model of Participation Programs

The field of participation programs in work organizations as has been revealed up to the present is vast, rich, diversified, and changing. In this organizational zoo, we can find a huge variety of participation animals in countless forms of cohabitation in organizational environments. We have discussed so far the main species in their main ecosystems. We turn now to an attempt to construct a general framework or model for the emergence, behavior, and performance of any participation program. The key concept in building such a model is looking at participation programs as open systems. Following Katz and Kahn (1966, 19–47), Buckley (1967, chaps. 4, 5), and Miller (1972), participation programs are conceptualized as open systems, living in organized environments, which provides them with input resources. These resources are processed and transformed into products, which are useful contributions to the environment and are exchanged for new inputs. By these assumed systemic relationships, the approach to participation programs is not merely instrumental. A participation program is not just another managerial or political tool. It is composed of people, information, jobs, skills, expectations, and many other ingredients that constantly need resources in order to create useful products. It is a living system, not an inanimate organizational object—a procedure, a rule, or a vacancy structure. As a living system, any participation program depends on external inputs, which are processed and digested by internal throughput devices into contributions, which are exported to the environment.

Chapter 9

System Elements of Participation Programs

INPUTS: GOALS

The first input element of participation programs is goals. Goals have an impact on the strategic and operational level. They define the expectation level of the participants and the vision horizon of the program. Goals serve to legitimize and provide a working framework for the participatory efforts. However, they are effective only when they exhibit a certain mix—difficult to measure—of desired values, utilities, and realistic expectations of the participants. Values and utilities are often agreed upon before the program starts. Expectations, however, are a more elusive element, and are sensitive to changing influences and to the cost that the participants are prepared to pay for goal attainment. For example, Strauss and Rosenstein (1970) and Derber (1970) concluded that many of the participation programs of the first generation did not meet the expectations of both the participants and the supporters. Rus (1970) reported that decreased commitment to participation was found, ironically, among activists more than among nonactivists in the Yugoslav system. Walker (1974, 24–25) suggested, at the same time, that positive reactions would be expected only in participation programs that would offer realistic opportunities for participation in combination with an appropriate value orientation. Otherwise, he predicted formalism (opportunities without desire for participation), frustration (desire without opportunities), and apathy (the lack of both). Blumberg (1968, 132) reiterated Likert's warning that when the amount of participation is less than or very much greater than expected, an unfavorable reaction is likely to occur. Substantially greater amounts of participation than expected appear to exceed the skills of employees to cope with it, and the best results are obtained when the amount of participation is somewhat greater than expected but still within the capacity of employees to effectively respond.

Bertch (1973, vol. 6, 71–85) examined this relative deprivation thesis and the application of this thesis to the Yugoslav self-management system between 1947 and 1972. He found four groups: *satisfied, nondeprived participants*—a small minority of workers, whose expectations grew with their managerial skills; *frustrated participants*—workers in advanced industries, whose growing expectations were not met and were blocked by institutional and political barriers; *frustrated nonparticipants*—highly skilled workers with potential for managerial roles, who missed their opportunities in the new system of self-management; and *satisfied nonparticipants*—workers from the agrarian sector with no self-management. Their general attitude toward the system was apathetic.

In a different context of American employees in an industrial setting and in a school, Alutto and Belasco (1972) found similar findings among three groups: participation-deprived, participation-saturated, and participation-balanced. The most frustrated were the participation-deprived and the participation-saturated employees.

The basic difference is between goals that emphasize participation as an end in itself, and goals that emphasize participation as a means to other ends, such as productivity or employees' satisfaction. Goals of participation as a desired way of life, regardless of their immediate instrumental utility, perhaps produce more frustration and relative deprivation than instrumental goals that are realistic and suitable to short-run expectations and capabilities of the participants. Instrumental goals characterize most of the participation programs in the second generation.

INPUTS: SUPPORT

The second input element is the support of important organizational constituencies for the program. Supportive constituencies are constantly a necessary condition for the program's survival and contribution. The well-known conclusion of Wagner (1994) about the small (though significant) effect of participation on employees' performance and satisfaction is also related to supportive constituencies. Eaton (1994) argued that it is unlikely that the average profit-maximizing employer would adopt and continue to use participation programs on moral grounds alone. So, the risk of erosion of employers' support is possible in any participation program. Examining the same problem from a different point of view, Schwochau et al. (1997) found that managers perceived greater support for their planned change from employees covered by participation or profit-sharing programs than from other employees.

Obviously, the legitimization of the program is enhanced by the supportive base of the participation program and the number of constituencies, but not necessarily by the consensus on the program's goals. On the contrary, the joining of multiple groups to the support network of the program diversifies qualitatively and quantitatively the goals and the vested interests, with the possible result of reduced consensus. In a study in the framework of an EI program, Tjosvold (1998) found that competitive goals were negatively correlated with the outcomes of productivity and employees' commitment to reduce costs. Earlier, however, Leana and Florkowski (1992) found that participation programs could have a number of objectives, with the possible lack of congruency or even built-in conflict of goals. But, for the program itself, what mattered was practical support rather than consensus.

INPUTS: PARTICIPANTS

The third input element is participants. They are mainly from the rank-and-file employees and from managers. Other participants may come from outside groups, such as suppliers, customers, and government authorities. Employees are supposed to be the major beneficiaries (Locke and Schweiger, 1979; Miller and Monge, 1986). However, to be effective, rank-and-file participants need information and experience. The participation literature offers ample evidence that employees tend to avoid ritualistic and sterile meetings, and lose interest and motivation without real opportunities for information sharing, learning, free exchange of views, and influence.

Another problematic sector of participants is middle managers and supervisors. Some observers noticed the neglect of this group in participation programs (Parnell and Bell, 1994). Recently, Fenton-O'Creevy (1998), in a survey of 155 organizations, examined the role of middle managers in EI programs in the United Kingdom. It was found that positive outcomes of employee involvement were lower in organizations that experienced middle management resistance. The study supports the view that middle managers may resist employee involvement practices in response to threats to self-interest (managerial status and job loss). This sometimes severely increases the resistance when middle managers feel that senior management support for EI is a threat to their positions.

Still, the effective size and composition of the participant body is a problem in any participation program. In a classic study in several dozen organizations, Hage and Dewar (1973) found that the values of a broad group of influential persons in the organization—the organizational elite—predict a success of organizational change better than formal structural parameters, or even better than the attitudes of the formal leader (director, CEO, and so on.).

THROUGHPUTS: PARTICIPATORY PRACTICES

Organizations cannot directly transform the ideas, information, and support inputs into desired contributions without a change in the culture of the nonparticipatory organization. Intermediate processes in the system are required to create and enhance participatory practices or routines. These practices create an organizational culture of participatory norms and a climate of sharing, and thereby make the difference between participatory systems and traditional ones.

Clarke et al. (1972, 6–8) defined a range of participation practices: consultation, collective bargaining, and self-management. Heller and Rose (1973) suggested five styles of decision-making—from unilateral managerial nonparticipatory style to unilateral employees' nonparticipatory style, with consultative and co-management styles in the middle. Knudsen (1995, 8–13) suggested four practices of employee participation: information sharing, consultation, co-determination, and unilateral employee decision-making. It seems that the most common participatory practices are information sharing, consultation, co-management, and self-management.[1]

Information Sharing

Sharing information is essential to any participatory culture, because information is the raw material for decisions and performance. However, information sharing is an asymmetrical and unilateral action, either by reporting to employees, or by feeding back to management, This participatory practice has low intensity and very often the informed people are passive in the process of information transmission. Reporting to employees is practiced typically before or after decisions are already made. This is a low-cost routine, and is best practiced when decision-makers want to avoid possible difficulties and prevent resistance to the proposed decisions. Participants in events of information sharing are not required to invest time and efforts in creating, processing, and preparing the information.

When correctly communicated, information sharing saves considerable time and misunderstandings in later stages of decision-making and implementation. However, information sharing as a participatory practice has its own weakness, which derives from the fact that the informer has almost total control of the process. Management, for example, has full control over releasing selective information, withholding undesired information, and presenting information in biased ways in order to persuade or calm the audience. Asymmetry may even increase in the interaction between professional skillful and well-versed informers and passive and less well-equipped employees (Clarke et al., 1972, 115–118; Mulder, 1971, 1973). On the other hand, lower participants have their own control over vital information, which is rarely reported in nonparticipatory culture. Therefore, despite its obvious benefits, information sharing alone does not safeguard against manipulative tendencies among information holders.

In a study of information-sharing systems in two companies in New South Wales, Australia (Hainey, 1984), 350 employees were presented with a range of information types and asked whether they wanted to receive that type of information. They were also asked to rate the quantity and quality of each type of information received. The results of the study indicated that employees were far from being satisfied with the information-sharing systems introduced and their subsequent participation in decision-making within the companies. However, there was sufficient support for the positive outcomes of the systems.

A special form of information sharing is *resistance*. This is the ability of participants (employees, supervisors, and so on.) to use de facto veto power in the face of a perceived or real damage to their interests, even in a participatory interaction. The ability of the system to contain certain legitimate veto power is a sign of maturity and responsiveness to participants' needs, and a built-in balancing mechanism. Resistance potential in a participatory culture differs from veto power in traditional industrial relations, because it is used before decisions are made. So, this is a proactive rather than a reactive practice. It has advantages over consultation in its low cost. On the other hand, veto power in a participatory culture cannot be used frequently, because it might exhaust the mutual trust between management and employees. It also requires collective action, which is not easy to mobilize.

Consultation

This is a more complicated practice. The interaction of consultation is bidirectional and mutual. It consists of more than a simple ad hoc chain of a stimulus pulse, followed by a response pulse. The participants are required to achieve higher intensities of interaction. Consultation involves a considerable degree of information sharing, but it goes further in eliciting ideas, feedback, critique; soliciting alternative solutions to problems; and building consensus around the proposed decisions and organizational policy.

This practice has three elements: a commitment of time, limits on the number of effective participants, and the professional skills required to deal with the issues. Consultation is cumbersome, and in complex issues it is almost impossible to consult with many participants without the heavy cost of untimely decision-making. On the other hand, employees tend to avoid consultative meetings on marginal and trivial issues. It is also important to recall that, under the practice of consultation, employees are not ultimately responsible for the policy or decisions that are made. So it seems that consultation, which requires investment of time and effort, is not well balanced by appropriate responsibilities. The paradox is that employing good practice of joint consultation brings employees closer to the decision-making power center, but not close enough to make the decisions. On the other hand, for managers, the temptation to remove "real issues" from the consulting agenda is sometimes too strong.

This is a vicious circle that has disrupted many joint consultation programs. The solution is to focus the consultation process on its effectiveness zone: limit the number of participants and number of meetings, train the participants for consultation skills, and concentrate on relevant issues that are manageable.

Co-Management and Self-Management

Co-management and self-management include the practices of information sharing and consultation. In addition, they include intensive formal and informal procedures and interactions for joint decision-making in a wide range of managerial issues. The degree of participation in these practices is, of course, higher than in former practices in terms of investment of responsibilities, time, and skills.

Employing self-management practices with a continuous, regular, and heavy load of time and responsibilities is possible only for operational issues in direct participation programs. On the other hand, comanagement practices are more viable in representative programs, which also have information sharing and consultation practices.

Other Aspects of Participatory Practices

From a behavioral point of view, participatory practices exhibit three basic modes: (a) presence, which means passive attendance in information-sharing forums and optional resistance rights, (b) active participation in decision-making on the job or via the work group (OJGP), and (c) active participation in decision-making (PDM).

Mere presence is the least intensive practice. Participants invest time, but withhold exertion of skills, abilities, and efforts beyond the required minimum. However, presence is often what is most effective. This is the case in many routine tasks or in situations of formal representation of organized interests. Sometimes being a passive participant, who guards the rights of individuals and groups by veto power, is even more effective than other modes of participation. By exhibiting presence behavior, individuals respond only to a certain minimum of the system's demands. Such behavior secures for them normal rewards and prevents organizational harassment. Also, not all employees can or want to participate more intensively even in return for appropriate rewards. For them, intensive participation threatens other interests in or out of the employing organization.

Participation on-the-job or in the group (OJGP) is more intensive participation. Participants not only invest time but also physical, mental, and emotional efforts beyond the duties of mere cooperation in interdependent tasks. Work systems can impose presence and functional cooperation, but they cannot motivate direct participation without attempting at least partially to meet the expectations, needs, and goals of employees. Since OJGP requires individual efforts and commitment beyond some required level, more congruence should exist between individual and system's goals. This often is addressed by consultation practices, or by arrangements of teamwork and self-directing jobs and groups.

Participation in decision-making (PDM) enhances participants' power and influence as they become partners in setting goals, planning, and operative decision-making, which is the objective ideally sought in co-determination or co-management practices. However, this practice does not match everyone's skill and will. Sagie and Koslowsky (1994), contrary to the bon ton of the empowerment ideal, provide evidence that employees respond more favorably to opportunities for participation in tactical rather than strategic issues. This is also related to managers' propensity to accept subordinates in decision-making roles (Hespe and Wall, 1976). Cotton et al. (1976) explored specific effects of PDM in different contexts and found that managers accept PDM if it is useful for their goals. Analyzing the ideal of empowerment, Mankin et al. (1997) restated what G. D. H. Cole said many years ago, that even in the best of circumstances, participation will be limited by the number of people who can be effectively involved in a decision: "When everyone participates, nothing gets accomplished."

Another issue of participatory practices is entropy, or chronic tendencies of disintegration. Even with sufficient inputs, participatory practices face chronic problems (Walker, 1976, 30–36). Participants experience built-in role conflict because of:

1. Their duties as carriers of management or organizational responsibilities beyond their normal duties as employees
2. Poor communication among participants, who perform under norms of participatory practices and nonparticipants
3. Tendencies of participatory practices to become marginal and ritualistic activities rather than effective and instrumental behaviors
4. Difficulties in diffusing participatory practices to the entire working community in the workplace

Thus, creating and maintaining participatory practices are not trivial endeavors, and merely setting up organizational structures and rules cannot accomplish the task. It requires vision, leadership, communication skills, experience, and other subtle properties of managing innovative projects.

OUTPUTS: SURVIVAL AND CONTRIBUTIONS

The final product is a series of performance targets that participation programs are supposed to improve. Productivity, rewards, quality of work life, and the like are benefits that justify the continuance of support, information, and commitment. Some stakeholders may be satisfied merely with participatory practices. This approach is typical of some labor unions, political leaders, and social thinkers, who value participation as a worthy end for its own sake. However, there is a strong expectation in work organizations that participation will contribute, not just survive; in other words, survival is a precondition to contribution.

Survival

Participation programs in the first generation—those that were driven by political and industrial relations strategies—have existed for quite a long time in comparison with the longevity of programs in the second generation. Among the few longitudinal studies, Griffin (1988) reported that many improvements produced by EI programs dropped back to their initial levels after 18 months. Other researchers reported a fairly high failure rate of QCs, QWL programs, and TQM/CQI programs within a relatively short time (see Drago, 1988; Eaton, 1994).

Contributions

How do we assess contributions of participation programs? In a classical book, Thompson (1967, 85–88) suggested three tests for organizational performance: efficiency test, when quantitative cost/benefit analysis is feasible; instrumental test, when organizations can measure a goal's attainment but are unable to "price" the success; and social test when goals and means are not well known or defined. In this case, referees subjectively do performance assessment.

Efficiency or instrumental tests are not applicable for most participation programs, because these programs lack clear definitions and standards of goals and means. For example, even in organizations that run formal and well-defined programs, it is difficult to assess what part of the overall performance is related to the participatory practices and what is the result of other activities. Thus, by default, the social test is the only feasible one. Nevertheless, the character of participation programs and their sensitivity to participants' expectations and behavior make the social test not merely a second-best tool. The participants are not just biased assessors. Their assessments are a key to the success or failure of such programs (Walker, 1976, 30–36).

Successful implementation of participation programs may lead to high performance, because employees, under good practices of participation, are supposed to be motivated to contribute skills and knowledge in their firm's interests and avoid shirking. However, participation programs have their own transaction costs associated with more decision-makers being involved and greater required communication among these participants (Levine and Tyson, 1990; Kelley and Harrison, 1992). Also, in the short run, price competition from lean production and/or low-wage firms may weaken participatory firms (Applebaum and Batt, 1994).

Direct participation programs that focus on job issues and link compensation to worker efforts significantly increase productivity. The broader the scope of participation, the greater its effect. Programs that give employees only informational and consultative roles, like quality circles, are ineffective and tend to be short-lived. Team production has high potential to increase productivity, but often is combined with changes in work organization, job security, compensation, and union-management relations. Therefore, it is difficult to isolate participation effects from the effects of other changes.

Using meta-analysis, Doucouliagos (1995) synthesized the results of 43 published studies to investigate the effects on productivity of various forms of worker participation: worker participation in decision-making, codetermination, and various forms of economic participation. He found that codetermination is negatively associated with productivity, but profit sharing, worker ownership, and worker participation in decision-making are all positively associated with productivity.

In another survey, Juravich (1996) concluded that the impact of EI programs had been mixed. The most consistent finding is that the greatest effect of EI programs is changes in attitudes: improved communications, job satisfaction, and improved labor-management relations. Even so, these improvements in worker attitudes are limited.

At the end of the 1980s, Cotton et al. (1988, 8–22) ignited a debate on the performance of participation programs. They reached two basic conclusions: First, that the effects of participation on satisfaction and performance varied according to the form of participation, and second, that all in all, the effects on performance are positive and significant. Leana, Locke, and Schweiger (1990) responded with an in-depth critique of Cotton and his associates. They dismissed their typology of participation programs as an inadequate classification framework. Wagner (1994) attempted to resolve the participation and/or performance issues by applying meta-analytic techniques to 11 other reviews of the participation literature. His results suggested that participation could indeed have statistically significant effects on performance and satisfaction, but that the average size of these effects is so small as to undermine its practical significance. Ledford and Lawler (1994) and Cotton (1995) responded to Wagner by saying that the narrow conclusion he reached is most likely a correct one: Limited participation has limited effects. However, the problem is that when the definition of participation is so narrow, it cannot have a major impact on organizational performance or employee well-being.

Kling (1995) found, in a survey of the effects of profit sharing on productivity, in 26 econometric studies, that a majority of the statistical tests showed a significant positive correlation between profit sharing and productivity. Productivity was generally 3 to 5 percent higher in firms with profit-sharing plans than in those without. In another study in 112 manufacturing firms in the framework of IMPROSHARE,[2] he found that defect and downtime rates fell 23 percent each in the first year after the scheme was introduced. The presence of either profit sharing or gain-sharing was found to be associated with higher productivity in an analysis of 841 manufacturing establishments in five Michigan counties. The magnitude of these effects varied from an average increase of 5 to 25 percent, depending on whether the firm was unionized, used work teams, or both.

NOTES

1.   Note that on this level of analysis, the terms *co-management* and *self-management* are used to describe specific behavioral modes rather than whole programs or other institutionalized and formal arrangements.

2.   A program of gainsharing in which workers are essentially paid bonuses equal to one-half of any increase in productivity.

Chapter 10

A Core Model of Participation Programs

The five system components of any participation program are arranged and presented in Figure 10.1, as a conceptual path model.[1] The components are ordered in a sequence of input variables, throughput variables, and output variables. The input variables are goals, participants, and support; the process or throughput variable is a set of participatory practices, and the output is contributions of the participation program. The assumed interaction between the *goals* and *participants* in the program (managers, employees, facilitators, and so on.) is well documented throughout this book. The *support* variable may relate, but not necessarily, to the *participants*. It comes from the higher echelons in the organization, or even from external constituencies, such as labor unions or government—levels that are normally remote from the actual carriers of the program.

The input variables lead to the throughput variables, the *participatory practices*. In this part of the system, the purposeful efforts, support, skills, and motivation of the participants are transformed into *contributions*. However, as mentioned earlier, for some programs, the *support* component has impact not only on the *participatory practices* but also directly on the *contributions*. This is common, for example, where participation programs are set up with technological improvement programs, and both types of programs are supported by the same organizational coalition.

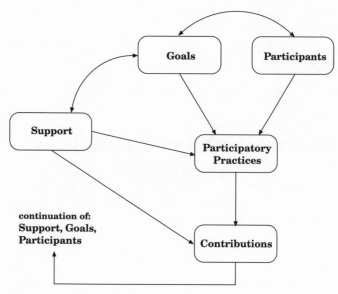

FIGURE 10.1.   *A model of a participation system.*

THE CONTEXT OF PARTICIPATION PROGRAMS

The participation system is embedded in work organizations, which are the source for its inputs and the market for its outputs. I propose to decompose this organizational environment into four "context areas": *strategy, individual, organizational,* and *performance.* The embedment of the participation program in its context environment is presented in Figure 10.2 (the bold arrows indicate assumed impacts of the context area on the participation program).

Strategy Area

This is where visions, missions, and business policy are created and shaped. Participation in work organizations has been always a strategic issue—either as a part of the entire organizational strategy or as a counter strategy by some agents or stakeholders (labor, intellectuals, politicians). Drago (1998) argued that EI programs were one of the strategies that employers use to play with workers' limited autonomy for their own profit-making interest. Indeed, it can be argued that workers' participation in low-level decisions provides them with a sense of involvement without endangering managerial control and

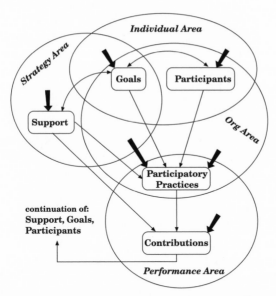

FIGURE 10.2.   *A participation program in its organizational context.*

profits.[2] Locke, Kochan, and Piore (1995) saw the whole issue of workplace participation as a changing global strategy toward decentralization and greater flexibility in work relations and deployment of labor.[3] In the 1960s and 1970s, management and labor strategy in many countries was to advance industrial peace and industrial democracy by creating indirect representative programs. The economic and technological turbulence of the last decades, with massive downsizing and outsourcing of human resources, left labor unions with a dilemma: to resist or to cooperate with the new management-initiated EI programs. Verma and McKersie (1987), Verma (1989), and Leana and Florkowski (1992) observed negative consequences for unions that adopted a strategy of noninvolvement. Cooke (1992) found that EI programs improve product quality, especially when management and unions jointly run the program, but not when the union remains uninvolved. Allen and Van Norman (1996) found that union opposition and adversarial labor-management relations chilled employees' interest in the EI activities and reduced their satisfaction and organizational commitment. Labor response, like management response, is thus an important strategic factor in any participation program.

However, on the company level, participation programs are often treated on an ad hoc basis, unplanned and in an opportunistic manner by both management and labor. This is not a straightforword and linear process, but rather a complex, often intuitive, and erroneous set of decisions and nondecisions—not necessarily ordered or planned in advance. This means that the strategy area is unstable even in the short run. De Sitter et al. (1997) proposed on this level two basic opposing strategies. One strategy is greater bureaucratization, avoiding participation, and making organizations complex and jobs simple. The second strategy is to reduce internal control by participatory management and make organizations simpler and jobs more complex.

Individual Area

In this area the human assets of the organization are deployed. The will and skill of individual participants—as employees or as managers—are a crucial factor for participation programs. The disposition of individuals to contribute their physical, mental, and emotional resources to their employing organization through participation should not be taken for granted. This individual disposition was never supported unequivocally. However, Freeman and Rogers (1994) found, as Blumberg (1968) did 30 years earlier, an enormous participation gap between what [American] workers desire to be involved in and what they are currently allowed to be involved in. Freeman and Rogers also provided information on workers' preferences regarding the form and structure of participation. Among other things, workers would like the right to elect representatives and to have access to company information, and they don't want management-dominated programs with little worker control. Instead what they want is a real voice in the workplace. However, there is a lot of variance among employees and managers as to the amount and forms of desired participation. Also important is the amount and composition of the human capital of the workforce. In detailed case studies of 72 companies, Bassi (1995) discovered that among manufacturing and nonmanufacturing firms that were implementing programs such as TQM, QCs, and work teams, the firms that established workplace education programs reported noticeable improvements in their workers' abilities and the quality of their products.

Organizational Behavior Area

This is the arena of group dynamics, organizational communication, organizational commitment, leadership patterns, and so forth. This is, of course, the most relevant context for a participatory culture. Parnell and Bell's survey of literature (1994) indicated solid positive relationships between participation and satisfaction, self-esteem, loyalty, and positive supervisor-subordinate relations. Indeed, most participation programs are established to solve organizational behavior issues. Managers, for example, see motivation and commitment of the workforce as important reasons to support participation programs. Indeed, many participation programs were set up to tackle these two issues. Low organizational commitment with its symptoms of high rates of turnover, absenteeism, tardiness, low morale, and sabotage is sometimes the first catalyst for an employer to adopt participatory solutions. In the well-known paradigm of Albert Hirschman (1970), participation, as an active collective and organizational means to arrest system deterioration, is a form of Voice. The other individual and nonparticipatory solutions that may prevail in the organizational area are Exit, Loyalty, or Neglect (Rusbult et al., 1986; Withey and Cooper, 1989).

Another variable in this context area is organizational climate, which might enhance or impede the creation of participatory practices. Unfortunately, it is hard to know which direction it might take. Tesluk et al. (1995) studied, in an American sample of 252 employees and first-level supervisors, the extent to which the knowledge and skills learned in EI program training were generalized beyond specific EI activities. The training was in participative decision-making, problem-solving, team skills, and quality control. The researchers reported that greater generalization of EI training to the job was found in those units where organizational climate did *not* support employee participation. The pre-existing favorable climate for employee participation was related negatively to generalization.[4]

The subtle character of participatory practices was well demonstrated in a study by Marchington et al. (1994), who explored the meaning of participation, perceived by 800 participants in various EI programs in 18 organizations in the United Kingdom, by means of an attitude survey and a series of in-depth case studies. They found no correlation between the range of EI practices that were in operation and the attitudes of employees participating in these practices. It was apparent that more participation practices did not imply a greater effect. Employees at two of the organizations with the greatest number of schemes held significantly different attitudes to EI. Moreover, employees at one organization were no less positive than those at another, despite the fact that patterns of EI at the former were much less prominent than at the latter. Furthermore, practices with the same title varied considerably in terms of their operational characteristics. Contrary to some claims that increased levels of EI lead to cultural change and improved levels of employee commitment to the organization, the authors suggested that EI is as much affected by the prevailing organizational culture as it is by a source of change.

Performance Area

In this area the results of participation programs are enhanced or impeded by a variety of environmental factors. Batt and Appelbaum (1995) found differences in performance of participation programs across occupations, organizational departments, and technologies. Doucouliagos (1995) found a stronger correlation between participation and performance among firms owned and controlled by workers than among capitalist firms adopting one or more EI practices, such as QCs. Juravich (1996) and Cooke (1994) argued that successful performance of EI programs is related to the intensity of the program, as measured by the frequency of meetings and the number of employees involved. In highly competitive, low-wage, and flexible nonparticipatory practices of employment, an EI program must be even more intensified to prevail in the traditional nonparticipatory environment. Another factor in the performance area is the nature of the industrial relations. Kelly and Harrison (1991) reported that EI programs are significantly more successful in unionized settings. However, given the mixed impact of EI on economic performance, EI is more likely to succeed in financially sound companies (Juravich, 1996).

Overlapping Areas

As one can see in Figure 10.2, the four context areas partially overlap, and thus create cross-sectional areas. This means that some elements of the participation program are exposed selectively and simultaneously to several organizational contexts, with the plausible contradictions and interactive effects (the major impacts are indicated by bold arrows in Figure 10.2). Goals and support should be most sensitive to the strategy area. The inclusion or exclusion of participation in the organization's agenda signals loudly and clearly the priority of the organization and its level of support for participation. Participants are exposed to the individual area where levels of personal motivation and skills are determined. However, they are also the major players in the organizational area. Personal goals of participants should be compatible, to a certain extent, with the program's goals. After all, individuals (both managers and employees) are also the carriers of the new participatory culture. Therefore, the intersection of the individual area with the organizational area is obvious.

Participatory practices, almost by definition, live or die in the organizational area. Nevertheless, their function as transformers of behavior into contributions makes them susceptible to the performance area, as well. Thus, participatory practices are exposed constantly to "radiation" of demands and pressures from the performance area, and this happens in the intersection of the organizational area and the performance area.

Contributions are supposed to result from the concerted efforts of the program's operation, and then to be exported to the organization, as indicated by the lowest arrow in the model. However, as noted earlier, the participation program is not the sole factor, and the contributions are also bound to external technological and economic strengths, weaknesses, opportunities, and threats (SWOT) in the performance area.

DEVELOPMENT AND DISINTEGRATION OF PARTICIPATION PROGRAMS

So far, we have modeled static states of participation programs. In this section we describe some dynamic processes in participation programs. The analysis will focus on two types of processes: development and disintegration.

Development Processes

Kochan and Dyer (1976) suggested three stages in a successful implementation of cooperative programs: an initial stimulus, a decision of both parties to participate, and maintenance of the parties' commitment. The decision to cooperate involves each side weighing the perceived costs and benefits of cooperation. Further, each side tries to maximize outcomes by seeking the best combination of adversarial and cooperative behavior (Cooke, 1990). Generally, this process has two approaches: *top-down development* and *bottom-up development*.

Top-Down Development

Development of participation programs in a top-down manner is presented in Figure 10.3. The initiation of the project starts at the apex of the organization. In the first stage (I), conditions in the strategy and individual areas emerge, and the major stakeholders build support, define common goals, and mobilize individual motivation. Typical actors in this stage are top managers and/or labor leaders, who indoctrinate their vision and the expected benefits of participation programs. A major difficulty at this stage is sometimes the indifference of employees and managers and their suspicions of the sincere intentions of the upper echelons.

In the second stage (II), if successful, forces in the organizational area are ripe for a change in creating the required participatory practices. The process is easier for organizations with a history of collaboration and trust between labor and management. However, for traditionally rigid, hierarchic and bureaucratic organizations, it is much more difficult to achieve.

In the third stage (III), the new participatory efforts are routinized (become "a way of life"), and effective management of the performance demands is attained. Note that performance in this stage may be hampered if the coalition of forces in the other areas is not strong enough. This happens when strategic, individual, and organizational determination among the stakeholders is insufficient or equivocal. But even with unequivocal alignment of forces in the context areas and participatory practices that are working well, the desired contributions may not result, due to uncontrollable externalities. For example, the QWL project in Shell UK from the mid-1960s to the early 1970s was reanalyzed by Blackler and Brown (1981). They revealed that despite early optimistic reports, the project and its achievements soon faded.

Bottom-Up Development

Development of participation programs in a bottom-up manner is presented in Figure 10.4. In the first stage (I), the project is initiated locally, often by some work groups or departments. The drive for initiating a participation scheme is normally the acknowledgment of both low-level management and employees of the mutual benefits of a participatory mechanism to solve local problems in the performance area. This initiative is enhanced by supporting, trusting, and encouraging people in the organizational area. In the second stage (II), the initiation in one corner of the organization spreads to other parts and more people are involved. If successful, the participation endeavor gets the attention of higher management (III) and secures support and incorporation of the program in the organizational strategy.

Note that when a participation program evolves from bottom to top, the common goals are crystallized in an organic manner, from small

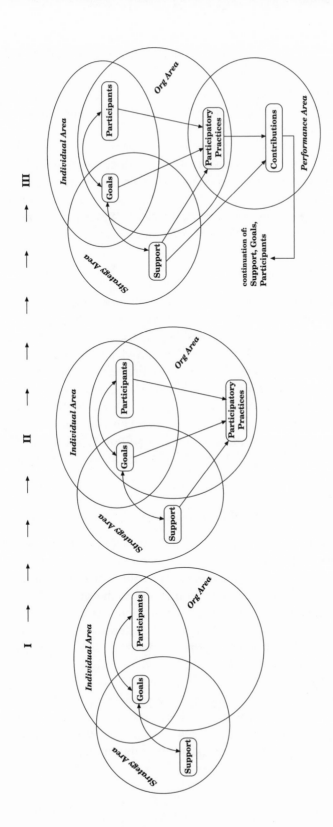

FIGURE 10.3. *Top-down development of a participation program.*

groups to the wider public in the workplace. In the top-down course, management has to indoctrinate its goals and to persuade employees in the mutual value of the program, where in bottom-up evolution, management takes a working arrangement that already has passed the performance test and legitimizes it. The problem of many bottom-up initiatives, however, is how to convince other people and departments to adopt the program, and thereby to gather the required momentum, that will be appreciated by top management. When this happens, the third stage institutes a full-fledged program.

Disintegration Processes

Processes of deterioration and disintegration occur when some parts of the program and/or its context functionally decline. Even though high rates of participation programs die and the reasons for their failure are well documented (Goodman, 1980; Lawler and Mohrman, 1985; Drago, 1988; Eaton, 1994), we can better understand the deterioration processes by the use of our model. There are many reasons for failures and shortcomings of participation programs. However, there are three recurrent processes of disintegration that cause a series of lapses: *detachment of the dominant coalition, deserting of participants,* and *atomization.*[5] These three types of disintegration are presented in Figure 10.5.

Detachment of the Dominant Coalition

This is a common occurrence when there is a loss of interest among the dominant coalition that supports the program. Creation of a supportive coalition is a major challenge in setting up any participation program. However, maintaining commitment to the program is perhaps even more difficult. The erosion of commitment can be predicted from a principal-agent theory. In participatory systems it becomes particularly difficult to convince management and other stakeholders to continue their support, as the free riding and shirking increase with the number of agents (Levine and Tyson, 1990). On the other hand, in unionized settings it is sometimes the union's side that demoralizes and impedes the program, when the union officials feel that they lose ground in the program (Cooke, 1994). So, the weak link in this disintegration is the support element (shaded in the model).

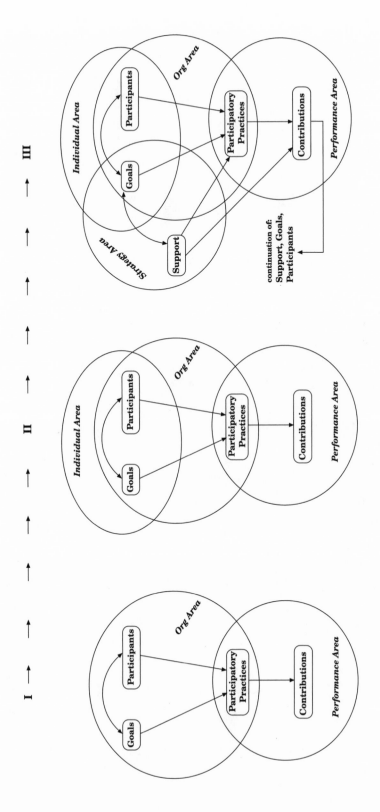

FIGURE 10.4. *Bottom-up development of a participation program.*

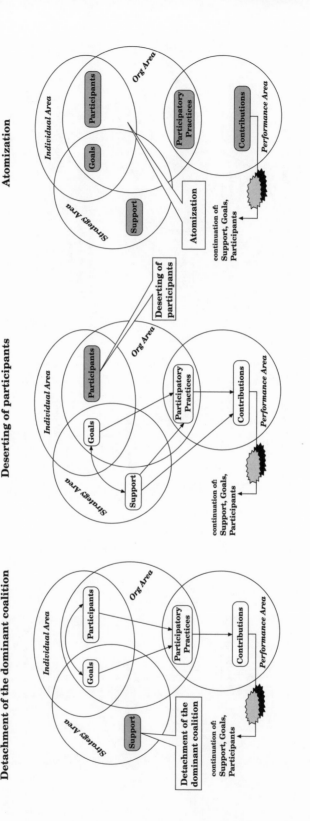

FIGURE 10.5. *Disintegration processes in participation programs.*

Deserting of Participants

Deserting of either employees or managers and supervisors is another cause of disintegration of participation programs. Baloff and Doherty (1989) discussed possible negative consequences for participant employees: they may be alienated by their peers who do not participate; managers may attempt to coerce them during participation, or managers may retaliate against them if the results of the participation displease them; they may have difficulty in adapting to old work practices in case of a terminated participation program; or they may even be discharged from the organization. Parallel detachment problems can be detected for managers and supervisors, as documented by Fenton-O'Creevy (1998). The weak link in this type of disintegration is the participants' element (shaded in the model).

Atomization

This type of breakdown occurs when several elements in the participatory system fall apart, and the metabolic relationships in the system decrease virtually to nullification. In this state the consensus on common goals vanishes, the support resources disappear or are diverted to different projects. the participants withdraw their commitment, and the participatory practices are ritualized and lose purposeful impact on the contributions. Such decline processes may characterize most of the reported failures of participation programs, which were not officially terminated.

NOTES

1.   Caine and Robson (1993) are close to my intentions in the term "model" (1993, 28): "A model can be considered as a simplified, but representative abstract of a real situation . . . models can be considered to be either descriptive or prescriptive in nature . . . In practice, a conceptual model is a diagrammatic representation of the problem situation and incorporates the use of techniques such as influence diagrams and flow charts . . ."

2.   The argument of Levine and Tyson (1990) is a variant of this approach. Also, see Osterman (1995), who explained how implementations of work/family and employee involvement programs are related to the employment strategy of firms, which seek to implement high-performance and/or high-commitment work systems.

3.   Some argued that Locke et al.'s study focused too much on the level of the enterprise and thus tended to underestimate the factors that shape workplace practices in countries with more centralized industrial relations institutions, such as the European countries.

4.   This is not a rare phenomenon, which sometimes occurs when the expectations for participation soar too high among employees who already have had experience with participation.

5.   The discussed three types of disintegration of participation programs are only a subset of a larger group of pathologies of participation programs. Further studies and elaboration of the model may reveal more types and forms of disintegration.

Chapter 11

Applying the Model to Specific Cases

In this section, the validity of the model is tested in two case studies: the performance of German works councils and the Israeli participation programs of the Histadrut. The general features of these programs have been described and discussed in previous chapters. The focus here is on explaining the dynamics of some aspects of these programs, with the assistance of the proposed model.

PERFORMANCE OF THE GERMAN WORKS COUNCILS

The performance of the German works councils was scrutinized in many German studies. There are also a few in-depth analyses in English. Freeman and Medoff (1984) defined the works councils as "collective voice." By offering the means to express discontent and increase productivity through collection of information about the preferences of the workforce, German works councils assist management in implementing a more efficient mix of wage and personnel practices. This, better human resource management lowers turnover, reduces hiring and training costs, and improves communication and workplace morale.

In a later study, Freeman and Lazear (1995) explained why neither employers nor unions would establish formal worker representation structures voluntarily. Employers are reluctant to grant workers sufficient representation rights and information about the firm that will increase productivity, because sharing this information increases the bargaining power of workers and permits workers to capture a larger share of the rents generated by the firm. They also argued that German works councils provide workers with increased job security, which fosters in workers a broader long-range perspective of the firm and greater readiness to exert efforts on its behalf. The job security argument received some support in a study by Sadowski, Backes-Gellner, and Frick (1995), who reported that job security was significantly higher in German firms with works councils. At the same time, however, increased job security and better information on the financial viability of the German firm enhance rent-seeking behavior on the workers' part, thus lowering the firm's profits. Freeman and Lazear believe that the German works councils will eventually offer a solution for this profit effect by decoupling pay from the factors that determine the size of the pie.

On the other hand, FitzRoy and Kraft (1987) argued that efficient firms do not need the bureaucratic impedimenta of works councils, and that they may be useful to some degree only for inefficient firms. Efficient firms can compensate for "under-provided participation" by means of advanced HRM practices, which include practices of direct participation. Addison (1996) countered that if the goal is indeed to decouple the factors of production and distribution, there would be no good reason for management to resist works councils. He concluded that Freeman and Lazear failed to recognize that the German works councils functioned, at least partially, as bargaining agencies.

The problem with the "collective voice" explanation, either in its pro-council version of Freeman and his colleagues or anti-council version of FitzRoy and Kraft, is that it ignores the organizational context of the works councils. Returning to the *organizational area* in our model, we may recall that in this area, voice behavior is part of a wider repertory of organizational commitment. However, German firms have used different routes to manage various modes of organizational commitment. For many years the German works councils exhibited voice behavior by employing PDM practices (information sharing and consultation) in the sense of Freeman and Lazear's model.[1]

On the other hand, management demanded and gained individual employee compliance with the firm's rules and individual Loyalty to its work ethics and performance objectives. Thus, in a German firm with a works council in the 1960s or 1970s, the Voice term in the equation was the domain of employees and their institutions, while the Loyalty term was the domain of management. The latter fostered Loyalty and work motivation by HRM practices of training, careers, rewards, benefits, and so forth. By separating voice behavior from loyalty behavior as two different facets of organizational commitment, the German firm was able to formulate a practical solution for both a firm's competitiveness and job security.

However, the new era of lean production, downsizing, and EI programs constrained the German works councils, as it did many other labor institutions elsewhere, to engage reluctantly in direct participation practices of OJGP. This change in strategy and practice is missing in Freeman and Lazear's model, and may cause a need to revise the theory. Extending activities of works councils to direct participation practices (OJGP) makes it a player in a managerial domain, where FitzRoy and Kraft discerned performance strength. Becoming a partner in managing OJGP programs, the works councils take part in a core managerial activity to improve performance objectives.

The differences between the works councils in their earlier time and in the last decades are depicted in Figure 11.1. In past years there was a constitutional and practical dissociation in German firms between the voice channel, which was dominated by labor through works councils, and the loyalty channel, which management dominated. In the second generation, works councils entered direct participation activities (OJGP) and thereby "invaded" management "territory" and shared the loyalty channel in addition to indirect participation in the voice channel. Success of labor in the loyalty channel may considerably increase employee motivation, productivity, and competitiveness of the firm. On the other hand, involving works councils in a decidedly managerial area of responsibility may disrupt the delicate triangle of unions, works councils, and management, since they may offset the gains of the voice channel by evoking low commitment behavior of exit, fence-sitting, and neglect instead.

THE ISRAELI PARTICIPATION PROGRAMS REVISITED

Using the participation path model, we can compare two extremely different participation programs in Israel. From the outset it can be stated that both programs were typically top-down endeavors. In the case of the JMCs, the Histadrut's political leadership created the necessary strategic alliances and then moved to institute joint consultation practices. In the case of the Social Program, Koor's management initiated the program and created its own alliances, and then designed detailed EI practices. Interestingly, even the decline processes of these

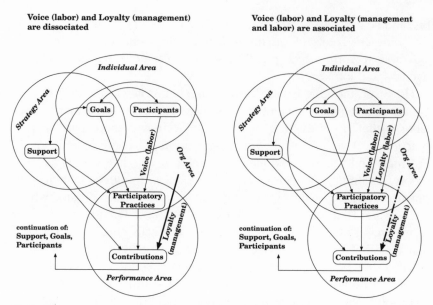

FIGURE 11.1. *Voice and loyalty in German works councils.*

programs were typical of top-down programs, namely, withdrawal from the programs and detachment of both political leaders and management groups. We can now return to internal mechanisms in these two programs.

By a statistical reanalysis of survey data, which was gathered in the 1970s and 1980s in two research studies, a comparison can be made of the five elements of the model in the two programs.[2] The measurement procedures are the same for the two studies. However, there are different items in some variables, due to a different time and context of each study, as is specified in Table 11.1.

The task of the researcher in this framework is to estimate and compare the weights of the paths or arrows in the model in Figure 11.2 for the two programs.[3] The arrows in Figure 11.2 describe the hypothesized causal relationships (a two-headed arrow marks an interaction relationship rather than a unidirectional one). However, only the statistically significant path coefficients were reported and marked by bolder lines. The fitting results are supplied as well. Both models fit the data with goodness of fit measures (other possible patterns of relationships, by omission or addition of arrows in the current set of five observed variables, yielded poorer goodness of fit for both programs).

TABLE 11.1. *Data for Two Israeli Programs*

	Joint Management Committees (WP)	Social Program (El)
Inputs		
Participants	5-item scale[i] (Cronbach α = .64)	3-category scale[ii]
goals	3-category scale[iii]	3-category scale[iii]
Support	6-item scale[iv] (Cronbach α = .67)	3-item scale[iv] (Cronbach α = .73)
Through puts		
Participatory practices	6-item scale[v] (Cronbach α = .91)	13-item scale[vi] (Cronbach α = .86)
Outputs		
Contributions	10-item scale[vii] (Cronbach α = .94)	12-item scale[vii] (Cronbach α = .91)

[i] Sample items: personal participation in JMC: initiates proposals, expresses opinions, prepares for JMC's meetings.
[ii] 1-unaware and not active, 2-aware of the program, but not active, 3-aware and active participant in the program.
[iii] 1-instrumental goals (participation as means), 2-mixed goals, 3-ideological goals (participation as end).
[iv] Sample items: who supports honestly the program: rank and file workers, shop committee members, managers.
[v] Sample items: We enjoy in the plant: reporting to workers on what is going in the plant by management, management consultation with workers, manaegment considers seriously workers' proposals, workers participate in management decisions.
[vi] Sample items: the program has impact on: personal willingness for social activity and involvement in the plant, personal willingness to put more effort on behalf of the plant, the power and position of the workers in the plant, the social relations with peers and supervisors, a real innovative change -not just lip service.
[vii] Sample items: the program contributes to: better labor relations, identification with the workplace, satisfaction, productivity, profitability, wages, less absences.

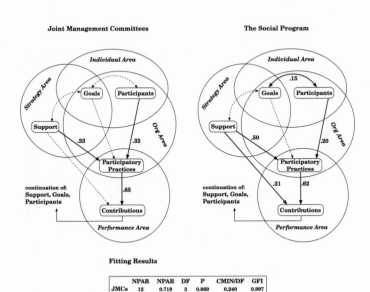

FIGURE 11.2. *Comparing two Israeli programs by a path model of participation programs.*

In both programs a strong effect was found to the path from participatory practices to contributions (0.65 and 0.62, respectively). This means that the core mechanism of the model has been validated in these cases: As long as the program has effective practices of participation, it produces positive organizational and personal contributions. The content and symbols of participatory practices in these two programs were different, but the effects on contributions were similar.

The different mechanisms in the two programs can be traced in the other parts of the model. As we can see in Figure 11.2, in the Social Program the impact of support on participatory practices is higher than in the JMCs (0.50 versus 0.33), while in the JMCs, the impact of participants is higher than in the Social Program (0.32 versus 0.20). These differences reflect the specific circumstances of each particular program: Management in the Social Program was more vigorous in enhancing productivity and QWL practices. In the JMCs, on the other hand, workers' delegates (but not other rank-and-file workers) participated ex officio more than the average participant in the Social Program did. Another difference between the programs is the significant direct effect of support on contributions in the Social Program (0.21), while in the JMCs this path is negligible. Again, management in the Social Program was more active in order to get results (contributions). In the JMCs, on the other hand, direct support for contributions was less important to the Histadrut's political officials.

A word on *goals:* In both programs *goals* had no effect on participatory practices. For the Social Program it is explained technically by a lack of variance (94.5 percent of the respondents defined the goals of the program in instrumental terms). However, the variance in the JMCs was greater and yet *goals* had no significant effect (46 percent indicated instrumental goals, 30 percent indicated mixed goals, and 19 percent indicated ideological goals). The observed isolation of goals (only a weak relationship with participants in the Social Program) raises the possibility that vision and mission statements of participation programs are less important than concrete interests and behavior of supporters and participants.

EVALUATING THE MODEL

The analysis of the two case studies, German and Israeli, which may reflect the experience of many other programs, suggests that supporters and participants behave in a similar way in a private competitive nonunionized setting as well as in a collective setting. Business and labor leaders eventually will be in the same boat, and have to cooperate in order to secure productivity, commitment, decent wages, and proper working life. The lesson from the Israeli case is that the "participation engine" is basically the same for different programs. However, it is not easy to generalize this finding. Participation engines need different "fuels" and different tuning for different programs. The nature of supporters and participants and the content of the participatory practices are changing from program to program and from generation to generation. A safer conclusion from the experience with many participation programs is that this engine does not work well under extreme conditions. We learned that turbulent environments hamper and even paralyze participation programs.

Participation programs in the first generation, namely, the first decades after World War II, flourished in relatively organized and calm economic and technological environments. Political and business leadership could respond effectively to environmental challenges by strategies of full employment and industrial democracy. However, in the last decades of the second generation the environment became much more competitive, global, and turbulent. In this context the corporatist policies of labor representatives on management boards and joint labor-management committees could not adequately face the new challenges.

Employee involvement programs in the second generation were part of the new strategies to enhance productivity and competitiveness, with new techniques of lean production, outsourcing activities, and privatization of the collective labor relations. In this framework, participation was pushed down from the strategic decision-making (PDM) to the operational work issues of teams and work groups. Labor unions lost many of their members and much of their power as partners to PDM programs.

These changes are reflected in the contents and styles of the three major inputs to participation programs: support, goals, and participants. Working under a changing context, these inputs enhanced new practices of direct participation on the job and/or group (OJGP), namely, teamwork and quality management. Not only was the strategy area changed but the individual area was changed as well. Employees of the last decades have been equipped with different knowledge, skills, abilities, and with different patterns of motivation and organizational commitment. In Europe, in particular, the new workforce has shown less interest in the older style of workers' participation in management, and in the United States employees have expressed an explicit desire to have greater involvement in the workplace.

Also, the performance area was changed. The advanced industrial countries moved quickly from the traditional industrial setting, the cradle of the first generation of participation programs, to high-technology industries and toward a service society. More and more employees have found themselves serving or supporting customers and "end-users" rather than producing physical products and commodities. For these service organizations, a different participatory culture is needed—a culture of direct involvement and teamwork because customers will not suffer bureaucrats and boring, unskillful, and unpleasant service providers. However, in a global cutthroat competition, with a growing virtualization of the workforce and the disappearance of job security and a sense of community, the newer participation programs, which have been initiated to cope with the "brave new world," are entering an extremely dangerous survival zone.

A further development and application of the proposed model should be directed toward constructing and refining diagnostic tools to monitor participation engines and their functioning in different context areas. Also, more development is needed to identify and describe growth and decline patterns of various engines.

NOTES

1. Drago and Wooden (1993), using survey responses from 249 managers from large Australian firms, found a strong positive linkage between voice and participation.

2. The data is taken from two studies by the author and colleagues: (1) Bar-Haim, A. (1979). "Workers' Participation in the Management of Industrial and Craft Plants." Work and Welfare Research Institute. The Hebrew University of Jerusalem (In Hebrew). Ninety-five workers' representatives and management delegates participated in this study. (2) Bar-Haim, A., Bar-Yosef, R., and Hochman, R. (1985). "The Social Program in Koor: An Evaluation Study in Five Plants." Work and Welfare Research Institute. The Hebrew University of Jerusalem (Hebrew). There were 709 employees who participated in this study.

3. The estimated parameters or coefficients are equivalent to standardized regression weights (bs). The model fitting was done by AMOS statistical package for Structural Equation Modeling (SEM), and was performed on the data in Appendix B. The residual or error terms, as required in structural equation modeling, were calculated, but are not presented.

Part IV

Future of Participation Programs

Since the day the Temple was destroyed, prophecy has been taken away from the prophets, and has been given to fools and infants.

—*Babylonian Talmud, Bava Batra 12b*

In this final part of the book, the discussion turns to speculations about the future of participation programs. Why should we enter into such a dubious business of clairvoyance? Here is the rationale. The historical analysis of two generations of participation programs shows dramatic changes over a relatively short period of 50 years. On the one hand, high volatility, a high mortality rate, and high fashionableness in forms and practices have characterized them, and make prediction a risky endeavor. However, the reasons for the attempts to forecast possible futures of participation programs are inherent in the very futurist orientation of participation in work organizations. The objects of inquiry have been limited in this book to participation in bureaucratic business and public organizations. Communes and cooperatives have been excluded (the Mondragon case in the appendix is an example of what is not discussed here). However, even in the noncommunal context, participation programs have always been more than managerial tools to improve productivity and work attitudes. They have been meant to change the world of work and to create a better future for employees and societies. At the extreme vision of work community à la Elton Mayo, participation programs could be a vehicle to solve the problems of the industrial civilization. This vision recurs again and again. At the other extreme of individualistic vision, participation programs could cure the alienation of the Marxian Homo Faber, and in between these two extremes lie many hopes and expectations for better quality of working life. Therefore, questions about the future of participation programs are closely related to the relevance and actuality of broader issues of our working life.

Nevertheless, in order to minimize the risk of prophecy, I use, in a free way, a technique known as "scenario planning" to analyze possible futures of participation programs. On the basis of past and present experience, we may try to stage "scenarios" of possible "futures" of participation programs. Scenario planning, as suggested by Wack (1985) and Schwartz (1991) is a disciplined method for imagining possible futures The method first used extensively by Royal Dutch/Shell in the 1970s as part of its process for generating and evaluating strategic options (Schoemaker and van de Heijden, 1992). This method has achieved global popularity with companies and even government agencies. In this method an attempt is made to reduce prediction errors by dividing solid knowledge from the unknown or uncertain knowledge. Various and even conflicting projections are made to stimulate thinking about yet unknown realities and to challenge the tendency to believe that the future will replicate the past.

Chapter 12

Preparing the Ground for Constructing Scenarios

Major steps in scenario planning are:

1. Assessing key features of past participation programs that remained active and relevant for their duration. These are the drivers of future scenarios.
2. Identifying uncertainties, which may determine and shape the opportunities and threats of participation programs.
3. Describing several future scenarios.

THE RELEVANCE OF PAST AND PRESENT DRIVERS

The past 50 years of participation programs shows first that there was a shift from indirect representative participation, with emphasis on managerial decision- making, to direct participation on the job or work group (OJGP), which has been focused on performance issues. Second, in both generations, economic and social results or contributions were achieved because of the dynamics of three basic intra-organizational drivers:

1. Support of top organizational agents—generally, management and labor and sometimes government agents as well.
2. Cooperation of expected participants—mainly workers, supervisors, and middle managers.

3. Participatory culture at the workplace—a set of behavioral customs, habits, and symbols, which enabled a spirit of joint efforts and cooperative behavior.

The external or environmental drivers, which shaped the dynamics of participation programs and determined the results ("contributions"), were different between the first and second generation. The first generation of indirect representative programs witnessed the power of organized labor, organized employers, and state governments in many countries, as we have described in the preceding chapters. On the local workplace level, support was composed of top captains of industry, top labor leaders, and top government officials. The participants (the representatives in the various works councils and corporate organs) were the elite of local workers and management, and the devised culture was permeated with social and political faiths, even at the expense of economic and performance efficiency. My guess is that these combined drivers will not prevail in the near future. Global competition, the collapse of the older international bipolar structure, privatization, and the information revolution destroyed the collectivist institutions of industrial relations that enabled the corporatist alliance between industrial elites in participation programs.

The second generation of direct participation programs was developed on the background of different drivers, which restructured the context and the content of participation programs. First, the economic conditions worsened both locally and internationally. Second, the world entered an era of fast-rising, new technologies, mainly information technology. Third, the postwar global order of the two superpowers collapsed and a new global economic and political order emerged. These changing factors made obsolete the older workers' participation programs. Work organizations found themselves fighting for survival. They needed technological and business restructuring with different markets, different required human skills, different sizes, and different modes of working with suppliers and customers. Labor unions were no longer able to provide the two basic goods of their raison d'être: job security and decent standards of working and living. The leadership of participation programs has moved from political and labor leaders to owners and managers. The latter were not interested in labor representatives on their boards or in other decision-making bodies, especially under the new regime of downsizing and outsourcing.

Was participation relevant under these conditions? Yes, of course, but in different terms. Going globally lean and mean dictated the parameters of the new participation programs. The supporters were mainly corporate management, not the whole industry or economy. Local labor leaders were dragged behind or were reluctant to cooperate with the new managerial programs. Participants came from rank and file and from the shop floor teams and work groups. However, the new techniques of teamwork and quality management required profound changes of practices and behavior among middle managers and supervisors, who lost responsibilities and authority. There was a limit to their will to cooperate, and also a limit to employees' will to intensify quality work just for autonomy and teamwork, and without additional adequate monetary compensation.

My guess is that the external drivers of technology, especially information technology, and virtualization of trade and work relations will continue to exert their impact on work organizations and participation programs. I do not doubt that the globalization process, as we know it today, will change. It also seems to me that the future of current regimented quality management programs, which "enforce" participation in teams and groups will not survive in the near future.

Can we learn about the future of participation programs from their performance in the last 50 years? The most conspicuous result is the high mortality rates of participation programs. The indirect representative programs, especially where they are mandatory by law, such as in Germany, are more enduring. However, most programs suffer deterioration and/or termination and do not survive longer than several years. The reasons are many, but the typical reasons are the detachment of the support agents, the desertion of participants, and the atomization of the programs' components. I believe that this feature of participation programs will not change in the near future.

Nevertheless, many programs have served their purpose even partially and for a short time. It is well known that at least in postwar Europe, in former Yugoslavia, in some developed countries, and in Israel, representative programs significantly contributed to industrial and social peace and to steady and smooth growth of productivity and national economy. The net contributions of the second-generation programs (when we control for factors such as technology and economic markets) are probably positive, but small. However, if we take single components such as teamwork and self-managing groups, the contribution to restructuring of work organizations and modernization of work systems is much more profound and widespread.

Whether teamwork and self-managing groups will continue to play a central role in future participation programs remains to be seen. Our skepticism in this matter stems from the observation that the new network arrangements of work enable many nagging aspects of real autonomous or semi-autonomous groups to be bypassed.

My provisional conclusion is that, at present, we can count on two constant forces or drivers that will continue with a high degree of certainty to determine and shape work organizations, and thus, participation programs, in the near future:

D1: Technologization, namely, equipping work life with excessive tools, information, and communication processors.

D2: Virtualization of relationships in work and labor relationships. This means that many more work organizations will work in cyberspace, from a distance, in many geographical locations, in complicated networks of communication rather than in closed and well-defined hierarchical systems.

In terms of strategic analysis, organizations will experience high-speed and high-intensity processes of acquisition and usage of tools and products of high technology. Second, they will extend their use of virtual networks for communication and work. These drivers alone will create new and vast sources of opportunities and threats for organizations. For example, Shostak (1999) analyzed eloquently both the threats and the opportunities of information technology, the Internet, and the virtualization for labor unions and labor relations.

KEY UNCERTAINTIES

Uncertainties are unknown or unsure determinant factors in the future. I identify three key uncertainties:

U1: Globalization. In its 276th Session (November 1999), the International Labor Office (ILO) defined globalization as a phenomenon with economic, political, and cultural dimensions. The economic dimension has been defined there as a process of rapid economic integration between countries. It has been driven by the increasing liberalization of international trade and foreign direct investment, and by freer capital and labor flows. Economic globalization manifests itself through an intensification of activities in international trade in goods and services, in capital and labor flows, in an increasing role of multinational enterprises, in the reorganization of production networks on an international scale, and in the adoption of new technologies, including information technology.

All these globalized systems, subsystems and processes that we know today may continue to function as they do, namely, to increase economic competition, giant mergers, and global partnerships at the expense of local—national and community—transactions and relationships. However, globalization may be shaped by a different modus operandi and different rules of the game. For example, the international community may be mobilized to curb and reduce the huge human and environmental costs of unrestrained globalization. Another possibility is that local communities will employ their political power to regulate globalization. The point is that globalization, in my view, is not a taken-for-granted driver of the future.

U2: Localization. Localization is the opposite process of globalization. It is a process of liberalization and encouragement of local (national and community) trade and capital flows, the use of local production networks, and the adoption of new technologies, including information technology for strengthening local products, local work communities, local cultures, and local traditions of work and management.

Its status as an uncertain factor of the future is obvious. Predicting successful localization process in the face of vigorous globalization may seem strange if not pathetic. However, this very weakness of localizatiom makes its prediction nontrivial.

U3: Democratization. Democratization is the extension process of democratic principles of governance from civil society to work organizations by power sharing, participation in decision-making, transparency of information, preservation of human rights, and so forth. Note that localization and democratization are not necessarily correlated. It is possible to have active processes of localization without democratization, as we may see in some countries, which vigorously nurture their local economy and culture, but neglect or even block democratic reforms in their institutional infrastructure. On the other hand, in democratic countries the drive to protect the local economy and local way of life stems from the need to respond to the demands of political parties and pressure groups in the democratic game.

In summary, I identify two major drivers (current forces that will prevail with a high probability in the near future): higher technologization of work organizations, and higher virtualization of management, work arrangements, and communication modes. I also identify two major uncertainties (current or future forces whose strength and direction are uncertain): shape and strength of globalization, localization, and democratization.

Chapter 13

Future Scenarios of Participation Programs

We have defined five environmental forces: two drivers that almost certainly will continue to exert their heavy impact on the context areas of participation programs and the programs themselves, and three uncertainties that may or may not continue to influence the context areas of participation programs. Scenarios in our case are several patterns of possible relationships among future combinations of drivers and uncertainties and future combinations of participation programs in their context areas. This framework is charted in Figure 13.1 as a sliced outer circle for the drivers and uncertainties and a sliced inner circle for the participation programs in their context areas. The task now is to examine these patterns or profiles as possible future scenarios.

SCENARIO 1: GLOOMY FUTURE FOR PARTICIPATION

D1: High technologization.
D2: High virtualization.
U1: High globalization.

U2: Low localization.
U3: Low democratization.

Given the strength of technology, virtualization, and globalization (see shaded areas in the outer circle in Figure 13.2), and given the

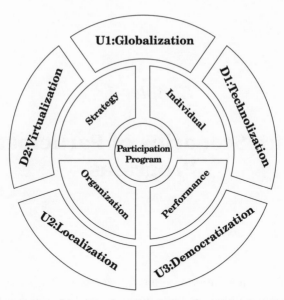

FIGURE 13.1.   *Future drivers and uncertainties of participation programs.*

weakness of localization and democratization forces, participation programs will continue to suffer high rates of mortality, no clear agenda, and opportunistic response to managerial fads of quasi participation. The unrestrained globalization with fast virtualization and technological change will accelerate forces of downsizing and outsourcing, will continue to weaken labor unions as partners in participation programs, and will weaken top management commitment to participation in a wild world of mergers and takeovers. On the level of the workplace, the global turbulence will restrict the readiness of individual participants to cooperate and to participate, and the cost of participation will be in terms of excessive material remuneration because of the shortage of social and emotional gratification. Participatory culture under this scenario will be weak, and the contributions of the programs will be overwhelmed by the nonparticipatory policies in the strategy area, and the nonparticipatory practices in the performance area (see shaded areas in the inner circle in Figure 13.2).

SCENARIO 2: BRIGHT FUTURE FOR PARTICIPATION

D1: High technologization
D2: High virtualization

FIGURE 13.2. *Scenario 1—gloomy future of participation programs.*

U1: Moderate globalization

U2: High localization
U3: High democratization

Given that globalization will be restrained and moderated, and that localization and forces of democracy will prevail (see shaded areas in the outer circle in Figure 13.3), participation programs will be able to thrive in more comfortable conditions. Technology and virtualization will serve participatory strategy and culture as well. For example, a lot of information sharing, consultation, and co-determination can be done in virtual networks of employees both via the Internet or the organizational intranet. Curbing the negative faces of globalization will begin a renaissance for participation programs from a better starting point—more flexible, more compatible with advanced technology, especially information technology, and in a more enlightened society and global environment. Actually, the roots of this vision are well developed in the socio-technical and the QWL movements. It also will fit well the political agenda of the new social democracy. The combination of technology, localism, and democracy will shape three of four context areas of participation programs:

FIGURE 13.3. *Scenario 2—bright future for participation programs.*

- Strategy area, in which socio-technical and new social-democratic policies will be advanced
- Individual and organizational behavior areas, where rich and sophisticated mixtures of individual competencies, motivation, and behavior will
  fertilize participatory cultures, and will enable fruitful contributions (see
  the shaded areas in the inner circle in Figure 13.3).
- However, the impact on the fourth area, the performance area, is incon-
  clusive in this scenario, since unknown factors will operate in this area
  and determine the end results.

Nevertheless, since participation in this scenario is an end in itself,
and since the general mood of this scenario is of a renaissance of social
responsibility, there is no reason to forecast negative results anyway.

SCENARIO 3: REASONABLE FUTURE FOR PARTICIPATION

D1: High technologization.
D2: High virtualization.
U1: High globalization.
U2: High localization.

U3: Low democratization.

FIGURE 13.4. *Scenario 3—reasonable future of participation programs.*

Given, as in Scenario 2, that globalization will be restrained and moderated, and localization will prevail, but not democratization (see shaded areas in the outer circle in Figure 13.4), a reasonable future is waiting for participation programs. They will enjoy the more comfortable conditions, as in Scenario 2 ("the bright future"). The processes of localization will counterbalance the pressures of globalization. However, the difference from Scenario 2 is the lack of parallel democratization processes. Localism with no democratic culture will encapsulate participation programs to limited issues and scopes, and will not infringe or threaten the existing nondemocratic industrial elite. Thus, participation will remain an instrumental device rather than a new culture and a new way of working life. In the context of participation programs, we will discover that strategy, individual, and performance areas will be relatively favorable to participation. However, the participatory culture will be rather weak, with a low level of personal involvement and more calculative commitment rather than a value orientation toward participation (see the shaded areas in the inner circle in Figure 13.4).

SCENARIO 4: PLURALISTIC FUTURE FOR PARTICIPATION

D1: High technologization.
D2: High virtualization.

U1: High globalization.
U2: High localization.
U3: High democratization.

Scenario 4, where all the drivers and uncertainties are high—more technologization and virtualization, more globalization and localization and democratization—poses a challenge to our prophecy exercise. Although not all the conditions have the same odds, all of them will act on work organizations simultaneously. In that case, which is charted in Figure 13.5 by shading all the areas in the outer circle, we cannot anticipate a coherent strategy for participation programs. All the context areas of participation programs, except for the strategy area, will actively enhance successful programs. This is because, under a simultaneous impact of all the forces, participation programs will have many niches of opportunities in the forms of human talents and motivation. They will be able to build advanced work communities with a sense of togetherness and democratic participation, and they will be benefited by the advanced technology and learning system in the efforts to contribute significant products and services.

However, in contrast with the bright Scenario 2, the complex, sometimes confusing, and dialectical nature of this scenario does not permit

FIGURE 13.5. *Scenario 4—pluralistic future of participation programs.*

to lean merely on success futures of participation and ignore the worst situations. This scenario depends on different states of equilibrium among all the forces in different countries, communities, and organizations. Such blessed balanced states, which enable real participation, do not emerge spontaneously. As in the past or in the present, people will have to desire it strongly and fight for it in the future.

Chapter 14

Epilogue

Our journey in the land of participation programs was enlightening, but also painful. I cannot say that I am now able to resolve the enigma and the fuzziness of the theme of participation. I am, however, convinced that work organizations desperately need participation on all levels. Participatory energy is perhaps the scarce commodity of our time. In real participatory processes, participants experience excitement and exhilaration, but also demands and exhaustion. The cost of participation is created by the cause of commitment, since commitment to a valuable goal requires a high investment of time, material, and personal resources. It also requires giving up other valuable goals. This is the dilemma of participants. In representative indirect participation programs, the few are requested for commitment. However, this participatory mode excludes the rest of the working community from the experience of participation. On the other hand, intensive direct participation is sometimes unrealistically demanded, and many employees may not be able or may not wish to immerse themselves intensively for a long time. The equilibrium state between too little and too much participation is not constant and is not easy to maintain, regardless of the ideological, political, and managerial colors of participation programs.

My conclusion deals with the questions What is best for participation programs, and what is my personal wishful thinking for participation programs? Starting with the second question, I wish participation would be a way of life in work organizations. Employees and managers should participate as much as they can and as much as they want. The objects of participation should be information, decisions, strategies, know-how, training, rewards, benefits, relationships, ownership, and the whole world of work. A participatory world of work, I believe, is a better world to live in.

Nevertheless, the best conditions for thriving participation programs are moderation and compromise. We know with sufficient certainty that cutthroat competitive environments or heavy and cumbersome bureaucracies are detrimental to participation programs. Furthermore, in contrast with what has been believed, participation programs are not practical alternatives to the destructive consequences of wild markets or unresponsive bureaucratic dinosaurs. Experience so far teaches us that participatory projects are the first to die under extreme conditions of market competition or bureaucratic fossilization.

Also the emerging new forms of network organizations, high-tech start-ups, Web-based companies, and nearly virtual organizations are not truly compatible with mature participation programs. In most of these rather small organizations, there are significant areas of "natural" participation in teamwork, in gainsharing, and in decision-making. However, their small size, their "ad-hocratic" character and their average short lives exclude them from being an arena for participation programs of real work organizations.

So, participation programs need "softer" environments, which are able to contain multiple and changing goals of individuals, groups, and organizational elite. They need a culture of tolerance, and, above all, they need recognition of and organizational opportunities for different levels of personal and group participation. Work organizations can develop a bagful of participation opportunities, which fits different capabilities and desires to participate. Employees and managers can participate in countless forms and doses. Participation programs require effort, skills, and resources, which in the right mixture can make sense of working and living.

Co-determination in German Coal, Iron, and Steel Industries

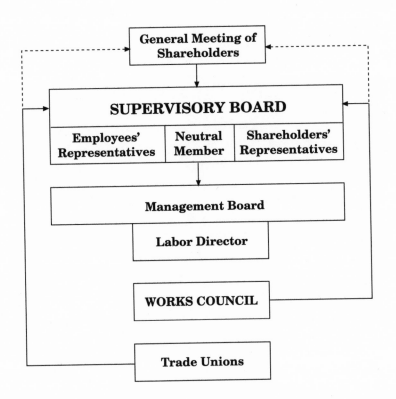

Appendix B

Data for Two Israeli Programs

THE JOINT MANAGEMENT COMMITTEES

Sample size=95

Correlations

```
 contributions 1.00
 p. practices   .69 1.00
 support        .34   .34 1.00
 goals          .10   .09 -.02 1.00
 participants   .24   .34   .06   .08 1.00
```

Means
```
  22.4 15.1 20.1 1.7 15.6
```
Standard deviations
```
  6.40 4.12 2.38 .79 2.77
```

THE SOCIAL PROGRAM

Sample size=404
Correlations
contributions 1.00
p. practices   .73 1.00
support   .53 .51 1.00
goals   -.01 -.05 -.06 1.00
participants .15 .21 .03   .15 1.00

Means
  29.0 33.6 11.8 1.1 1.7
Standard deviations
  9.47 4.91 1.92 .29 .68

Appendix C

"The Challenge of Mondragon"
George Benello*

As I mentioned at the beginning of the book, cooperatives are beyond the scope of this book. However, some excerpts from George Benello's assessment in the mid-1980s, "The Challenge of Mondragon" (in *Reinventing Anarchy Again,* edited by Howard Ehrlich (AK Press, San Francisco, 1996) are illuminating and helpful in understanding the cultural dimension of any participatory system, with its implicit problematic issues of imitation, adoption, and diffusion of successful models:

The [Mondragon] system [of cooperatives], which spreads throughout the surrounding Basque region, is named after Mondragon, a town in the mountains of Guipuzkoa Province near Bilbao. Since its start in the 1950s, it has gained an international reputation, with similar models now being developed in England, Wales, and the United States.

The first cooperative was founded by a Catholic priest, Don Jose Maria Arizmendi, who participated in the Spanish Civil War on the Republican side. In 1943 he founded an elementary technical school in Mondragon, and with several graduates of his school and a couple dozen other members, in 1956 he founded a small worker-owned and worker-managed factory named ULGOR, which produced kerosene stoves.

This cooperative venture proved successful and developed into the flagship enterprise of the whole system that later came into being. At one point, ULGOR numbered over 3,000 members, although this was

---

*Howard Ehrlich (Ed.) 1996. *Reinventing Anarchy Again*. AK Press.

later recognized as too large and was reduced. The structure of this enterprise served as the model for the latter enterprises forming the system. Following the Rochedale principles, it had one member-one vote; open membership; equity held by members and hence external capitalization by debt, not equity; and continuing education.

Three years after ULGOR was founded, Don Arizmendi suggested the need for a financial institution to help fund and give technical assistance to other start-up cooperatives. As a result, the Caja Laboral Popular (CLP), a credit union and technical assistance agency was founded. The CLP contains an Empressarial Division, with a staff of over 100, which works intensively with groups desiring to start cooperatives or in rare cases to convert an existing enterprise. It does location studies, market analysis, product development, plans the buildings, and then works continuously for a number of years with the start-up group until it is clear that its proposal is thoroughly developed and financially and organizationally sound. In return, the CLP requires that the cooperative be part of the Mondragon system, via a Contract of Association, which specifies the already proven organizational and financial structure and entails a continuing supervisory relation on the part of the CLP. The surplus of the industrial cooperatives is deposited in the CLP and reinvested in further cooperatives. This close and continuing relationship with the financial and technical expertise of the CLP is both unique and largely responsible for the virtually 100 percent success rate within the system.

The CLP is considered a second degree cooperative, and its board is made up of a mix of first level or industrial cooperative members and members from within the CLP itself. In addition to the CLP there are a number of other second degree cooperatives: a social service cooperative which assures 100 percent pension and disability benefits, a health care clinic, and a women's cooperative which allows for both flex-time and part-time work; women can move freely from this to the industrial cooperatives. Also there is a system of educational cooperatives, among them a technical college which includes a production cooperative where students both train and earn money as part-time workers. This, too, is operated as a second degree cooperative with a mixed board made up of permanent staff and students.

Mondragon also features a large system of consumer cooperatives, housing cooperatives and a number of agricultural cooperatives and building cooperatives. Today the total system's net worth is in the billions. Mondragon consists of 86 production cooperatives averaging several hundred members, 44 educational institutions, seven agricultural cooperatives, 15 building cooperatives, several service cooperatives, a network of consumer cooperatives with 75,000 members, and the bank. The Caja Laboral has 132 branches in the Basque region and recently opened an office in Madrid. This is significant, since it indicates a willingness to expand beyond the Basque region. The CLP's assets are over a billion dollars.

Mondragon produces everything from home appliances (it is the second largest refrigerator manufacturer in Spain) to machine tool factories and ferryboats, both of which it exports abroad. It represents over one percent of the total Spanish export product. With its 18,000 workers, it accounts for about five percent of all the jobs in the Basque country. It also produces high technology products. Its research institute, Ikerlan, regularly accesses U.S. data bases and has developed its own industrial robots for external sale and for use in its own factories. Mondragon has spent considerable time studying and implementing alternatives to the production line; its self-managed organizational system is now being complemented with the technology of group production.

The internal organization of a Mondragon cooperative features a General Assembly, which ordinarily meets annually and selects management. In addition there is a Social Council which deals specifically with working members' concerns. There is also a Directive Council, made up of managers and members of the General Assembly, in which managers have a voice but no vote. This system of parallel organization ensures extensive representation of members' concerns and serves as a system of checks and balances.

Mondragon enterprises are not large; a deliberate policy now limits them to around 400 members. To obtain the benefits of large scale, along with the benefits of small individual units, Mondragon has evolved a system of cooperative development. Here, a number of cooperatives constitute themselves as a sort of mini-conglomerate, coordinated by a management group elected from the member enterprises. These units are either vertically or horizontally integrated and can send members from one enterprise to the other as the requirements of the market and the production system change. They are able to use a common marketing apparatus and have the production capacity to retain a significant portion of a given market.

Mondragon productivity is very high—higher than in its capitalist counterparts. Efficiency, measured as the ratio of utilized resources (capital and labor) to output, is far higher than in comparable capitalist factories. One of the most striking indications of the effectiveness of the Mondragon system is that the Empressarial Division of Mondragon has continued to develop an average of four cooperatives a year, each with about 400 members. Only two of these have ever failed. This amazing record can be compared with business start-ups in this country, over 90 percent of which fail within the first five years.

Mondragon produces standard industrial products using a recognizable technology of production. It does not practice job rotation, and management is not directly elected from the floor—for good reason, since experiments elsewhere that have tried this have not worked. Members vary in the nature of their commitment. In fact there is something of a split in Mondragon between those who see Mondragon as a model for the world and those who prefer to keep a low profile and have no interest in proselytizing beyond their confines. Mondragon has also been faulted for failing to produce mainly for local consumption. It is in the manufacturing, not community development business, and, while it creates jobs, its products are exported all over the world. It has exported machine tool factories to eastern European countries, to Portugal and to Algeria; a Mondragon furniture factory is now operating in New York State. Mondragon does not export its system with the factories however; they are simply products, bought and run by local owners. In general, it makes little attempt to convert the heathens; at present, it is swamped by visitors from all over the world, and it finds this hard enough to deal with without going out and actively spreading the word.

Mondragon has awakened worldwide interest. The Mitterand government in France has a special cabinet post for the development of cooperatives, the result of its contact with Mondragon. In Wales, the Welsh Trade Union Council is engaged in developing a system of cooperatives patterned after Mondragon. In England, the Job Ownership Movement along with numerous local governments developed both small and large cooperatives on the Mondragon model. Progressives in the Catholic Church, seeing Mondragon as an alternative to both capitalism and communism, have helped establish industrial cooperatives in Milwaukee and in Detroit.

References

Abrahamsson, B. (1977). *Bureaucracy or Participation: The Logic of Organization.* Sage Publications: Beverly Hills, CA.

Adams, R. J. (1992). Efficiency is not Enough (A Need for More Worker Participation at Work). *Labor Studies Journal.* 17, 1, 18–28.

Adams, R. J., and Rummel, C. H. (1977). Workers' Participation in West Germany: Impact on the Worker, the Enterprise and the Trade Union. *Industrial Relations Journal.* 8, 1, 4–22.

Addison, J. T., Schnabel, C., and Wagner, J. (1996). German works councils, profits, and innovation. *Kyklos.* 49, 4, 555–582.

Adizes, I. (1971). *Industrial Democracy: Yugoslav Style: The Effect of Decentralization on Managerial Behavior.* Free Press: New York.

Adizes, I. (1972). On Conflict Resolutions and an Organizational Definition of Self-management. *First International Conference on Participation and Self-Management.* Dubrovnik, 13–17 December, Vol. 5, 7–33.

Allen, R. E., and Van Norman, K. L. (1996). Employee Involvement Programs: The Noninvolvement of Unions Revisited. *Journal of Labor Research.* 17, 479–495.

Alutto, J. A., and Belasco, J. A. (1972). A Typology for Participation in Organizational Decision-Making. *Administrative Science Quarterly.* 17, 1, 117–125.

Appelbaum, E., and Batt, R. (1994). *The New American Workplace: Transformation of Work Systems in the United States.* ILR Press: Ithaca, NY.

Argyris, C. (1973). Personality and organization: Theory revisited. *Administrative Science Quarterly.* 18, 2, 141–164.

Ashton, T. S. (1948). *The industrial revolution: 1760–1830.* Oxford University Press: London.

Bailey, J. (1983). *Job design and work organization.* Prentice-Hall: London.

Baillie, J. (1995). Exposing Out-of-date Ideals that Culture Gurus Hold Dear. *People Management.* 1, 47.

Baloff, N., and Doherty, E. M. (1989). Potential Pitfalls in Employee Participation. *Organizational Dynamics.* 17, 3, 51–52.

Barnard, C. I. (1966). *The Functions of the Executive.* Harvard University Press: Cambridge.

Barnard, C. I. (1970). Cooperation. In: Grusky, O., and Miller, G. A. (eds.). *The Sociology of Organizations.* The Free Press: New York.

Bassi, L. J. (1995). Upgrading the U.S. workplace: Do reorganization, education help? *Monthly Labor Review.* 118, 5, 37(11)

Batt, R., and Appelbaum, E. (1995). Worker Participation in Diverse Settings: Does the Form Affect the Outcome, and If So, Who Benefits? *British Journal of Industrial Relations.* 33, 3, 353–378.

Beekun, R. I. (1989). Assessing the Effectiveness of Sociotechnical Interventions: Antidote or Fad? *Human-Relations.* 42, 10, 877–897.

Bendix, R. (1956). *Work and authority in industry.* John Wiley: New York.

Bernstein, P. (1976). *Workplace Democratization: Its Internal Dynamics.* Kent University Press: Kent, Ohio.

Bertch, G. K. (1973). The Individual and Participatory Democracy in Yugoslavia: An Application of Relative Deprivation Theory. *First International Conference on Participation and Self-management.* Dubrovnik. 13–17 December. Vol. 6, 71–85.

Blackler, F. H. M., and Brown, C. A. (1981). A New Philosophy of Management: Shell Revisited. *Personnel Review.* 10, 1, 15–21.

Blauner, R. (1964). *Alienation and Freedom.* Chicago University Press: Chicago.

Bluestone, B., and Harrison, B. (1982). *The De-industrialization of America.* Basic Books: New York.

Blum, E. (1970). The Director and Self-management. In: Broekmeyer, M. J. (Ed.). *Yugoslav Workers' Self-management: Proceedings of a Symposium Held in Amsterdam,* 7–9 January. D. Reidel Publishers: Amsterdam.

Blumberg, P. (1968). *Industrial Democracy: The Sociology of Participation.* Constable: London.

Bolweg, J. F. (1975). Final Report on the International Management Seminar on Workers Participation. *OECD.* Versailles, 5–8 March.

Braun, E., and Senker, P. (1982). *New Technology and Employment.* Manpower Service Commission: London.

Buckley, W. (1967). *Sociology and Modern System Theory.* Prentice-Hall: New Jersey.

Caine, D., and Robson, A. (1993). Models for Decision-Making. *Management Services*. 37, 1, 28–30.

Cameron, K. S., Sutton, R. I., and Whetten, D. A. (Eds.). (1988). *Readings in Organizational Decline: Frameworks, Research, and Prescriptions*. Ballinger Publishing Company: Cambridge, MA.

Champagne, P. J., and Chadwin, M. L. (1983). Joint Committees Boost Labor Management Performance and Facilitate Change. *Advanced Management Journal*. 48, 3, 19–27.

Chell, E. (1983). Political Perspectives and Workers' Participation at Board Level: The British Experience. In: Crouch, C., and Heller, F. (Eds.). *International Handbook of Organizational Democracy*. Wiley: Chichester, UK.

Cherns, A. (1975). Perspectives on the Quality of Working Life. *Journal of Occupational Psychology*. 48, 3, 155–167.

Chesters, A. (1997). What You Need to Know About Works Councils. *Global Workforce*. July, 22–23.

Clarke, R. C., Fatchett, D. J., and Roberts, B. C. (1972). *Workers' Participation in Management in Britain*. Heinemann: London.

Co-determination in the Federal Republic of Germany. (1980). The Federal Minister of Labour and Social Affairs. West Germany.

Cohen, S. G., and Bailey, D. E. (1997). What Makes Teams Work: Group Effectiveness Research from the Shop Floor to the Executive Suite. *Journal of Management*. 23, 3, 239–290.

Cohen, S. G., Chang, L. C., and Ledford, G. E. (1997). A Hierarchical Construct of Self-Management Leadership and Its Relationships to Quality of Work Life and Perceived Work Group Effectiveness. *Personnel Psychology*. 50, 275–308.

Cole, G. D. H. (1957). *The Case for Industrial Partnership*. Macmillan: London.

Cole, G. D. H. (1975). Self-Management in Industry. In: Vanek, J. (Ed.). *Self-management: Economic Liberation of Man*. Penguin: Harmondworth, Middlesex, UK.

Collins, D. (1996). Case Study: 15 Lessons Learned from the Death of a Gainsharing Plan. *Compensation and Benefits Review*. 28, 31–40.

Cooke, W. N. (1990). Factors Influencing the Effect of Joint Union-Management Programs on Employee-Supervisor Relations. *Industrial and Labor Relations Review*. 43, 5, 587–603.

Cooke, W. N. (1992). Product Quality Improvement Through Employee Participation: The Effects of Unionization and Joint Union-Management Administration. *Industrial and Labor Relations Review*. 46, 1, 119–134.

Cooke, W. N. (1994). Employee Participation Programs, Group-based Incentives, and Company Performance: A Union-Nonunion Comparison. *Industrial and Labor Relations Review*. 47, 4, 594–609.

Cordery, J. L., Mueller, W. S., and Smith, L. M. (1991). Attitudinal and Behavioral Effects of Autonomous Group Working: A Longitudinal Field Study. *Academy of Management Journal.* 34, 2, 464–476.

Coser, L. A., and Rosenberg, B. (Eds.). (1976). *Sociological Theory: A Book of Readings.* 4th Ed. Macmillan: New York.

Cotton, J. L. (1993). *Employee Involvement: Methods for Improving Performance and Work Attitudes.* Sage: Newbury Park. CA.

Cotton, J. L. (1995). Participation's Effect on Performance and Satisfaction: A Reconsideration of Wagner. *Academy of Management Review.* 20, 2, 276–278.

Cotton, J. L., Vollrath, D. A., Froggatt, K. L., Lengnick-Hall, M. L., and Jennings, K. R. (1988). Employee Participation: Diverse Forms and Different Outcomes. *Academy of Management Review.* 13, 8–22.

Coxson, H. P. (1996). Workplace Cooperation: Current Problems, New Approaches—Comment on Delaney. *Journal of Labor Research.* 17, 63–68.

Crossland, C. A. R. (1963). *The Future of Socialism.* Schoken: New York.

Cummings, T. G. Self-regulating Work Groups: A Sociotechnical Synthesis. (1978). *Academy of Management Review.* 3, 625–634.

Dachler, H. P., and Wilpert, B. (1978). Conceptual Dimensions and Boundaries of Participation in Organizations: A Critical Evaluation. *Administrative Science Quarterly.* 23, 1–34.

Dar-El, E. M. (1986). *Productivity Improvement: Employee Involvement and Gainsharing Plans.* Elsevier: Amsterdam.

Davis, L. E., and Sullivan, C. S. (1980). A Labour-Management Contract and Quality of Working Life. *Journal of Occupational Behaviour.* 1, 1, 29–41.

Davis, L. E., and Cherns, A. B. (Eds.). (1975). *The Quality of Working Life.* The Free Press: New York.

De Sitter, L. U., den Hertog, J. F., Dankbaar, B. (1997). From Complex Organizations with Simple Jobs to Simple Organizations with Complex Jobs. *Human Relations.* 50, 5, 497–534.

Derber, M. (1970). Cross Currents in Workers' Participation. *Industrial Relations.* 9, 123–136.

Doucouliagos, C. (1995). Worker Participation and Productivity in Labor-Managed and Participatory Capitalist Firms: A Meta-Analysis. *Industrial and Labor Relations Review.* 49, 58–77.

Drago, R. (1998). Worker Participation in Capitalist Firms. In: O'Hara, P. (Ed.). *Encyclopedia of Political Economy.* Routledge: London and New York.

Drago, R., and Wooden, M. (1993). Do Union Voice and Worker Participation Coincide? A Study of Australian Managers' Perceptions. *Economic and Industrial Democracy.* 14, 4, 573–588.

Drago, Robert. 1988. Quality Circle Survival: An Exploratory Analysis. *Industrial Relations.* 27, 3, 336–351.

Dun, W. N. (1973). The Economics of Organizational Ideology: The Problem of Compliance Structure in Workers' Management. *First International Conference on Participation and Self-Management.* Dubrovnik, 13–17 December, Vol. 6, 195–220.

Eaton, A. E. (1994). The Survival of Employee Participation Programs in Unionized Settings. *Industrial and Labor Relations Review.* 47, 3, 371–389.

Eaton, A. E., and Voos, P. B. (1992). Unions and Contemporary Innovations in Work Organization, Compensation, and Employee Participation. In: Mishel, L., and Voos, P. (Eds.). *Unions and Economic Competitiveness.* M. E. Sharpe: Armonk, NY.

Edelstein, J. D. (1967). An Organizational Theory of Union Democracy. *American Sociological Review.* 32, 9–31.

Edosomwan, J. A. (1992). Six Commandments to Empower Employees for Quality Improvement. *Institute of Industrial Engineers*, 24, 7, 14–15.

Eitzen, D. S., and Zinn, M. B. (Eds.) (1989). *The Reshaping of America.* Prentice-Hall: Englewood Cliffs, NJ.

Emery, F. E. (1980). Designing Socio-technical Systems for "Greenfield Sites." *Journal of Occupational Behavior.* 1, 19–27.

Emery, F. E. (1982). New Perspectives on the World of Work: Socio-Technical Foundations for New Social Order? *Human Relations.* 35, 12, 1095–1122.

Emery, F. E., and Thorsrud, E. (1969). *Form and Content in Industrial Democracy.* Tavistock: London.

Euronline. (1998). *New European Survey Focuses on Workplace Innovation and Employment.* The European Foundation for the Improvement of Living and Working Conditions.

Farber, H. S. (1990). The Decline of Unionization in the United States: What Can Be Learned from Recent Experience. *Journal of Labor Economics.* 8, 1, Part 2, 75–105.

Fenton-O'Creevy, M. (1998). Employee Involvement and the Middle Manager: Evidence from a Survey of Organizations. *Journal of Organizational Behavior.* 19, 1, 67–84.

FitzRoy, F. R., and Kraft, K. (1985). Unionization, Wages, and Efficiency— Theories and Evidence from the U.S. and West Germany. *Kyklos.* 38, 493–504.

FitzRoy, F. R., and Kraft, K. (1987). Efficiency and Internal Organization: Works Councils in West German Firms. *Economica.* 54, 493–504.

FitzRoy, F. R., and Kraft, K. (1990). Innovation, Rent-Sharing and the Organization of Labour in the Federal Republic of Germany. *Small Business Economics.* 2, 95–103.

Flanders, A., Pomeranz, R., and Woodward, J. (1968). *Experiment in Industrial Democracy: A Study of the John Lewis Partnership.* Faber: London.

Florkowski, G. (1987). The Organizational Impact of Profit Sharing. *Academy of Management Review.* 12, 4, 622–636.

Florkowski, G. W., and Schuster, M. H. (1992). Support for Profit Sharing and Organizational Commitment: A Path Analysis. *Human Relations.* 45, 5, 507–523.

Freeman, R. B., and Rogers, J. (1994). Worker Representation and Participation Survey. *Princeton Survey Research Associates:* Princeton, NJ.

Freeman, R. B., and Medoff, J. L. (1984). *What Do Unions Do?* Basic Books: New York.

French, J. R. P., Israel, J., and Aas, D. (1960). An Experiment in Participation in a Norwegian Factory. *Human Relations.* 13, 3–10.

Fromm, E. (1955). *The Sane Society.* Reinehart: New York.

Furstenberg, F. (1978). Workers' Participation in Management in the Federal Republic of Germany. *International Institute for Labour Studies.* Research Series No. 32.

General Accounting Office (1987). *Employee Stock Ownership Plans: Little Evidence of Effects on Corporate Performance. GAO.* Washington, DC.

Geyer, F., and Heinz, W. R. (Eds.) (1992). *Alienation, Society and the Individual: Continuity and Change in Theory and Research.* Transaction Publishers: New Brunswick, NJ.

Glew, D. J., O'Leary-Kelly, A. M., Griffin, R. W., and Van Fleet, D. D. (1995). Participation in Organizations: A Preview of the Issues and Proposed Framework for Future Analysis. *Journal of Management.* 21, 3, 395–418.

Goodman, P. S. (1980). Realities of Improving the Quality of Work Life: Quality of Work Life Projects in the 1980s. *Proceedings of the Spring IRRA Meetings, Labor Law Journal.* August, 487–494.

Goodman, P. S., Devadas, R., and Hughson, T. L. (1988). Groups and Productivity: Analyzing the Effectiveness of Self-managing Teams. In: Campbell, J. P., Campbell, R. J., and Associates (Eds.). *Productivity in Organizations.* Jossey-Bass: San Francisco.

Gordon, J. (1992). Work teams: How Far Have They Come? *Training.* October: 59–65.

Grant, R. M., Shani, R., and Krishnan, R. (1994). TQM's Challenge to Management Theory and Practice. *Sloan Management Review.* 35, 2, 25–35.

Greengard, S., and Meissner, J. (1993). Don't Rush Downsizing: Plan, Plan, Plan. *Personnel Journal.* 72, 11, 64–73.

Grenier, G., and Hogler, R. L. (1991). Labor Law and Managerial Ideology: Employee Participation as a Social Control System. *Work and Occupations.* 18, 3, 313–333.

Griffin, R. W. (1988). Consequences of Quality Circles in an Industrial Setting: A Longitudinal Assessment. *Academy of Management Journal.* 31, 2, 338–358.

Gronning, T. (1997). The Emergence and Institutionalization of Toyotism: Subdivision and Integration of the Labour Force at the Toyota Motor Corporation from the 1950s to the 1970s. *Economic and Industrial Democracy*.18, 3, 423–455.

Gruneberg, M. M. (Ed.) (1976). *Job Satisfaction*. Macmillan: London.

Guest, D., and Knight, K. (Eds.) (1979). *Putting Participation into Practice*. Gower Press: UK.

Gulowsen, J. (1972). A Measure of Work-Group Autonomy. In: Davis, E., and Taylor, J. D. (Eds.). *Design of Jobs*. Penguin: Harmondsworth.

Gustavsen, B. (1992). Dialogue and Development: Theory of Communication, Action Research and the Restructuring of Working Life. Van Gorcum: Assen, The Netherlands.

Gustavsen, B., and Engelstad, P. H. (1985). The Design of Conferences and the Evolving Role of Democratic Dialogue in Changing Working Life. *Human Relations*. 39, 2, 101–116.

Hackman, R. J., and Oldham, G. (1980). *Work Redesign*. Addison-Wesley: Reading, MA.

Hackman, R. J., and Wageman, R. (1995). Total Quality Management: Empirical, Conceptual, and Practical Issues. *Administrative Science Quarterly*. 40, 309–442.

Hage, J., and Dewar, R. (1973). Elite Values Versus Organizational Structure in Predicting Innovation. *Administrative Science Quarterly*. 18, 3, 279–290.

Hainey, G. (1984). High Information Sharing Companies: What Their Employees Think. *Work and People*. 10, 1, 17–22.

Hammer, M., and Champy, J. (1993). *Reengineering the Corporation: A Manifesto for Business Revolution*. Nicholas Brealey: London.

Harari, O. (1997). Ten Reasons TQM Doesn't Work. *Management Review*. 86, 38–44.

Hartman, H. (1970). Co-determination in West Germany. *Industrial Relations*. 9, 1, 138–147.

Heller, F. A., and Rose, J. S. (1973). Participation and Decision-Making Re-examined. *First International Conference on Participation and Self-Management*. Dubrovnik, 13–17 December, Vol. 4, 123–133.

Hertog, J. F. D. (1977). The Search for New Leads in Job Design: The Philips Case. *Journal of Contemporary Business*. 6, 2, 49–67.

Herzberg, F. (1966). *Work and Nature of Man*. Crowell: New York.

Herzberg, F., Mausner, B., and Snyderman, B. (1959). *The Motivation to Work*. (2d Ed.). Wiley: New York.

Hespe, G., and Wall, T. (1976). The Demand for Participation Among Employees. *Human Relations*. 29, 411–428.

Hetterer, H. *The Two Factor Theory—The Economics of Reality*. Random House: New York.

Hirschman, A. O. (1970). Exit, Voice and Loyalty: Responses to Decline in Firms, Organizations and States. Harvard University Press: Cambridge, MA.

Hodson, R., Creighton, S., Jamison, C. S., Rieble, S., and Welsh, S. (1994). Loyalty to Whom? Workplace Participation and the Development of Consent. *Human Relations.* 47, 8, 895–909.

Horvat, B. (1971). Yugoslav Economic Policy in the Post-war Period: Problems, Ideas, and Institutional Developments. *American Economic Review.* 61, 3, Part 2, 1971, 69–169.

Huxley, R. C., and Robertson, D. (1997). *Just Another Car Factory? Lean Production and its Discontents.* Cornell University Press: Ithaca, NY.

Industrial Democracy in Europe International Research Group. (1981). *Industrial Democracy in Europe.* Clarendon Press: Oxford.

Industrial Democracy in Europe International Research Group. (1993). *Industrial Democracy in Europe Revisited.* Oxford University Press: Oxford.

Israel, J. (1971). *Alienation: from Marx to modern sociology, a macrosociological analysis.* Allyn and Bacon: Boston. .

Jacobi, O., and Hassel, A. (1996). Does Direct Participation Threaten the "German Model"? In: Regalia, I., and Colin, G. (Eds.) The Position of the Social Partners in Europe on Direct Participation. *Country studies.* Volume II. Working Paper No. WP/96/03/EN. Dublin, European Foundation for the Improvement of Living and Working Conditions.

Jessup, H. R. (1990). New Roles in Team Leadership. *Training and Development Journal.* November, 79–83.

Juravich, T. (1966). Empirical Research on Employee Involvement: A Critical Review for Labor. *Labor Studies Journal.* 21, 2, 51–69.

Katz, D., and Kahn, R. L. (1966). *The Social Psychology of Organizations.* Wiley: New York.

Kelly, M. R., and Harrison, B. (1992). Unions, Technology and Labor Management Cooperation. In: Mishel, L., and Voos, P. (Eds.). *Unions and Economic Competitiveness.* M. E. Sharpe: Armonk, NY.

King, C. D., and van de Vall, M. (1969). Dimensions of Workers' Participation in Managerial Decision-Making. *Industrial Relations Research Association.* 22, 164–177.

King, C. D., and van de Vall, M. (1978). *Models of Industrial Democracy: Consultation, Co-determination and Workers' Management.* Mouton Publishers: The Hague.

Klein, K., and Rosen, C. (1986). Employee Stock Ownership in the United States. In: Stern, R., and McCarthy, S. (Eds.) *The Organizational Practice of Democracy.* Wiley: New York.

Kling, J. (1995). High Performance Work Systems and Firm Performance. *Monthly Labor Review.* 118, 29–36.

Knudsen, H. (1995). *Employee Participation in Europe*. Sage: London.

Kochan, T. A., and Dyer, L. (1976). A Model of Organizational Change in the Context of Union-Management Relations. *The Journal of Applied Behavioral Science*. 12, 1, 59–78

Kochan, T. A., and Osterman, P. (1994). *The Mutual Gains Enterprise: Forging a Winning Partnership Among Labor, Management and Government*. Harvard Business School Press: Boston.

Kolodny, H., and Stjernberg, T. (1986). The Change Process of Innovative Work Designs: New Design and Redesign in Sweden, Canada, and the U.S. *The Journal of Applied Behavioral Science*. 22, 3, 287–301.

Kruse, D. L. (1993). *Profit sharing: Does It Make a Difference? The Productivity and Stability Effects of Employee Profit-sharing Plans*. Upjohn Institute for Employment Research: Kalamazoo, MI.

Lawler, E. E. (1996). Far From the Fad In-Crowd. *People Management*. 2, 38–40.

Lawler, E. E., and Mohrman, S. A. (1985). Quality Circles after the Fad. *Harvard Business Review*. 63, 1, 65–71.

Lawler, E. E., Mohrman, S. A., and Ledford, G. E. (1995). *Creating High Performance Organizations: Practices and Results of Employee Involvement and Total Quality Management in Fortune 1000 Companies*. Jossey-Bass: San Francisco.

Leana, C. R., and Feldman, D. C. (1992). *Coping with Job Loss: How Individuals, Organizations, and Communities Respond to Layoffs*. Lexington: New York.

Leana, C. R., and Florkowski, G. W. (1992). Employee Involvement Programs: Integrating Psychological Theory Management Practice. In: Feris, G., and Rowland, K. (Eds.), *Research in Personnel and Human Resources Management: A Research Annual*. JAI Press: Greenwich, CT, and London 10, 233–270.

Leana, C. R., Locke, E. A., and Schweiger, D. M. (1990). Fact and Fiction in Analyzing Research on Participative Decision-Making: A Critique of Cotton, Vollrath, Froggatt, Lengnick-Hall, and Jennings. *Academy of Management Review*. 15, 1, 137–146.

Ledford, G. E., and Lawler, E. E. (1994). Research on Employee Participation: Beating a Dead Horse? *Academy of Management Review*. 19, 4, 633–636.

Leiter, J. (1985). Work Alienation in the Textile Industry: Reassessing Blauner. *Work and Occupations*. 12, 4, 479–498.

Levine, D., and Tyson, L. D. (1990). Participation, Productivity, and the Firm's Environment. In: Alan Blinder (Ed.). *Paying for Productivity*. Brookings Institution: Washington, DC.

Lichtenstein, N., and Harris, H. J. (Eds.). (1993). *Industrial Democracy in America: The Ambiguous Promise*. Woodrow Wilson Center Press and Cambridge University Press: Cambridge.

Ligus, R. G. (1993). Methods to Help Reengineer Your Company for Improved Agility. *Industrial Engineering*. January.

Likert, R. (1961). *New Patterns of Management*. McGraw-Hill: New York.

Lipset, S. M., Trow, M. A., and Coleman, T. S. (1956). *Union Democracy: The Internal Politics of the International Typographical Union*. The Free Press: Glencoe, IL.

Liverpool, P. R. (1990). Employee Participation in Decision-Making: An Analysis of the Perception of Members and Nonmembers of Quality Circles. *Journal of Business and Psychology*. 4, 4, 411–422.

Locke, E., and Schweiger, D. M. (1979). Participation in Decision-Making: One More Look, In: Staw, B. M., and Cummings, L. L. (Eds.). *Research in Organizational Behavior*, 2. JAI Press: Greenwich, CT.

Locke, R., Kochan, T., and Piore, M. (1995). Re-conceptualizing Comparative Industrial Relations: Lessons from International Research. *International Labour Review*. 134, 2, 139–161.

Mankin, D., Cohen, S. G., and Bikson, T. K. (1997). Teams and Technology: Tensions in Participatory Design. *Organizational Dynamics*. 26, 63–76.

Marchington, M., Wilkinson, A., Ackers, P., and Goodman, J. (1994). Understanding the Meaning of Participation: Views from the Workplace. *Human Relations*. 47, 8, 867–894.

Marks, M. L., Mirvis, P .H., Hackett, E. J., and Grady, J. F. (1986). Employee Participation in a Quality Circle Program: Impact on Quality of Work Life, Productivity, and Absenteeism. *Journal of Applied Psychology*. 71, 61–69.

Martin, C. L., Parsons C. K., and Bennett, N. (1995). The Influence of Employee Involvement Program Membership During Downsizing: Attitudes Toward the Employer and the Union. *Journal of Management*. 21, 5, 879–890.

Maslow, A. H. (1943). A Theory of Human Motivation. *Psychological Review*, 50, 370–396.

Mayo, E. (1945). *The Social Problems of an Industrial Civilization*. Division of Research Graduate School of Business Administration, Harvard University: Boston.

McCaffrey, D. P., Faerman, S. R., and Hart, D. W. (1995). The Appeal and Difficulties of Participative Systems. *Organization Science*. 6, 6, 603–627.

McGregor, D. (1960). *The Human Side of Enterprise*. McGraw-Hill: New York.

Michels, R. (1962). Political Parties: A Sociological Study of the Oligarchical Tendencies of Modern Democracy. The Free Press: New York.

Miller, J. G. (1972). Living Systems: The Organization. *Behavioral Science*. 17, 1–182.

Miller, K. I., and Monge, P. R. (1986). Participation, Satisfaction, and Productivity: A Meta-analytic Review. *Academy of Management Journal*. 29, 727–753.

Millward, N. L., Stevens, M., Smart, D., and Hawes, W. R. (1992). *Workplace Industrial Relations in Transition: The ED/ESRC/PSI/ACAS Surveys.* Dartmouth Publishing: Aldershot, UK.

Mirkovic, D. (1987). Sociological Reflections on Yugoslav Participatory Democracy and Social Ownership. *East European Quarterly.* 21, 319–331.

Mitchell, D. J. B., Lewin, D., and Lawler, E. E. (1990). Alternative Pay Systems, Firm Performance, and Productivity. In: Blinder, A. S. *Paying for productivity: A look at the evidence.* Center for Economic Progress and Employment series. Brookings Institution: Washington, DC.

Mitchell, T. (1973), Motivation and Participation: Integration. *Academy of Management Journal.*16, 670–679.

Moldaschl, M., and Weber, M. M. (1998). The "Three Waves" of Industrial Group Work: Historical Reflections on Current Research on Group Work. *Human Relations.* 51, 3, 347–388.

Mouzelis, N. P. (1975). *Organization and Bureaucracy.* Routledge and Kegan Paul: London.

Mueller, H. E. (1999). Driving Change by Participation. *Die Mitbestimmung.* Hans-Bockler Foundation. Dusseldorf.

Mueller-Jentsch, W. (1995). Germany: From Collective Voice to Co-management. In: Rogers, J., and Streeck, W. (Eds.). *Works Councils-Consultation, Representation, and Cooperation in Industrial Relations.* University of Chicago Press: Chicago and London.

Mueller-Jentsch, W., Rehermann, K., and Sperling, H. J. (1992). Sociotechnical Rationalisation and Negotiated Work Organisation: Recent Trends in Germany. In: *New Directions in Work Organisation: The Industrial Relations Response.* OECD: Paris.

Mulder, M. (1971). Power Equalization Through Participation. *Administrative Science Quarterly.* 16, 1, 31–38.

Mulder, M. (1973). The Learning of Participation, *First International Conference on Participation and Self-Management.* Dubrovnik, 13–17 December, Vol. 4, 219–228.

Naftali, F. (1944). *Economic Democracy (Collected Papers).* Davar: Tel-Aviv (Hebrew).

Newton, K. (1978). Some Socio-Economic Perspectives on the Quality of Working Life. *International Journal of Social Economics.* 5, 3, 179–

Obradovic, J. (1970). Participation and Work Attitudes in Yugoslavia. *Industrial Relations.* 20, 163–169.

Olson, C. A. (1996). Works Councils: Consultation, Representation, and Cooperation in Industrial Relations. *Journal of Economic Literature.* 34, 4, 1979–1981.

Osterman, P. (1994). How Common is Workplace Transformation and Can We Explain Who Adopts It? *Industrial and Labor Relations Review*. January 1994, 173–188.

Osterman, P. (1995). Work/Family Programs and the Employment Relationship. *Administrative Science Quarterly*. 40, 681–700.

Ozaki, M. (1996). Labour Relations and Work Organization in Industrialized Countries. *International Labour Review*. 135, 1, 37–58.

Parks, S. (1995). Improving Workplace Performance: Historical and Theoretical Contexts. *Monthly Labor Review*. 118, 5, 18–28.

Parnell, J. A., and Bell, E. D. (1994). The Propensity for Participative Decision-Making Scale: A Measure of Managerial Propensity for Participative Decision-Making. *Administration and Society*. 25, 4, 518–530.

Parsons, T. (1951). *The Social System*. Free Press: Glencoe, IL.

Parsons, T. (1960). *The Structure and Process in Modern Societies*. Free Press: Glencoe, IL.

Pasmore, W. A. (1995). Social Science Transformed: The Socio-technical Perspective. *Human Relations*. 48, 1, 1–20.

Pasmore, W. A., and Fagans, M. R. (1992). Participation, Individual Development, and Organizational Change: A Review and Synthesis. *Journal of Management*. 18, 2, 375–397.

Pateman, C. (1970). *Participation and Democratic Theory*. Cambridge University Press: Cambridge.

Pearson, C. A. L. (1992). Autonomous Workgroups: An Evaluation at an Industrial Site. *Human Relations*. 45, 9, 905–936.

Pendleton, A., McDonald, J., Robinson, A., and Wilson, N. (1995). Patterns of Employee Participation and Industrial Democracy in UK Employee Share Ownership Plans. *Centre for Economic Performance Discussion Paper 249*. London School of Economics.

Peterson, R. B., and Tracy, L. (1992). Assessing Effectiveness of Joint Committees in A Labor-management Cooperation Program. *Human Relations*. 45, 5, 467–488.

Pollalis, Y. A. (1996). A Systemic Approach to Change Management: Integrating IS Planning, BPR, and TQM. *Information Systems Management*. 13, 19–25.

Pusic, E., and Supek, R. (1972). Forward. *First International Conference on Participation and Self-management*. Dubrovnik. 13–17 December. Vol. I. 5–7.

Rafaeli, A. (1985). Quality Circles and Employee Attitudes. *Personnel Psychology*. 38, 3, 603–615.

Ramsay, H. (1980). Phantom Participation: Patterns of Power and Conflict. *Industrial Relations Journal*. 11, 46–59.

Rice, A. K. (1958). Productivity and Social Organization The Ahmedabad Experiment: Technical Innovation, Work Organization and Management, Tavistock Publications: London.

Riesman, D. (1961). *The Lonely Crowd: A Study of the Changing American Character.* Yale University Press: New Haven.

Rigby, D. (1993). The Secret History of Process Re-engineering. *Planning Review.* 3/4, 24–27.

Rooney, P. (1988). Worker Participation in Employee-Owned Firms. *Journal of Economic Issues.* 22, 2, 451–458.

Rosenstein, E. (1977). Workers' Participation in Management: Problematic Issues in the Israeli System. *Industrial Relations Journal.* 8, 2, 55–69.

Ruiz-Quintanilla, A. S., Bunge, J., Freeman-Gallant, A., and Cohen-Rosenthal E. (1996). Employee Participation in Pollution Reduction: A Socio-technical Perspective. *Business Strategy and the Environment.* 5. (Special issue).

Rus, V. (1970). Influence Structure in Yugoslav Enterprises. *Industrial Relations.* 20, 163–169.

Rusbult, C. E., Johnson, D. J., and Morrow, G. D. (1986). Determinants and Consequences of Exit, Voice, Loyalty, and Neglect: Responses to Dissatisfaction in Adult Romantic Involvement. *Human Relations.* 39, 1, 45–63.

Sadowski, D., Backes-Gellner, U., and Frick, B. (1995). Works councils: Barriers or boosts for the competitiveness of German firms? *British Journal of Industrial Relations.* 33, 3, 493–513.

Sagie, A., and Koslowsky, M. (1996). Decision Type, Organizational Control, and Acceptance of Change: An Integrative Approach to Participative Decision Making. *Applied-Psychology: An International Review.* 45, 1, 85–92.

Sartory, G. (1965). *Democratic Theory.* Praeger: New York.

Shacht, R. (1970). *Alienation.* Anchor Books: New York.

Schneider, B., and Alderfer, C. P. (1973). Three Studies of Measures of Need Satisfaction in Organizations. *Administrative Science Quarterly,* 18, 4, 489–505.

Schwartz, P. (1991). *The Art of the Long View.* Doubleday: New York.

Schwarz, R. (1990–1991). Participative Decision-Making and Union Management Cooperative. Efforts. *Review of Public Personnel Administration.* 11, 38–54.

Schwochau, S., Delaney, J., Jarley, P., and Fiorito, J. (1997). Employee Participation and Assessments of Support for Organizational Policy Changes. *Journal of Labor Research.* 18, 379–401.

Seeman, M. (1959). On the Meaning of Alienation. *American Sociological Review.* 24, 783–791.

Sheppard, H. L., and Herrick, N. Q. (1972). *Where Have All the Robots Gone?* The Free Press: New York.

Shoemaker, P. J. H., and van de Heijden, C. A. J. M. (1992). Integrating Scenarios into Strategic Planning at Royal Dutch/Shell. *Planning Review*. 20, 41–46.

Shostak, A. B. (1999). *CyberUnion: Empowering Labor Through Computer Technology*. M. E. Sharpe: Armonk, New York.

Simon, H. A. (1976). *Administrative Behavior: A Study of Decision-Making Processes in Administrative Organization*. 3rd. Ed. Free Press: New York.

Sorensen, K. H. (1985). Technology and Industrial Democracy: An Inquiry into Some Theoretical Issues and Their Social Basis. *Organization Studies*, 6, 2, 139–159.

Spector, P. E. (1986). Perceived control by employees: A Meta-analysis of Studies Concerning Autonomy and Participation at Work. *Human Relations*, 39, 1005–1016.

Stambuk, V. (1985). Self-management Thirty-five Years Later. *Review of International Affairs*. 36, 29–31.

Stern, R. N. (1988). Participation by Representation: Workers on Boards of Directors. *Work and Occupations*. 15, 4, 396–422.

Strauss, G. (1982). Workers' Participation in Management: An International Perspective. In: Staw, B., and Cummings, L. L. (Eds.). *Research in Organizational Behavior*. (Vol. 5). JAI Press: Greenwich, CT.

Strauss, G., and Rosenstein, E. (1970). Workers' Participation: A Critical View. *Industrial Relations*. 9, 197–214

Strumthal, A. (1964). *Workers' Councils: A Study of Workplace Organization on Both Sides of the Iron Curtain*. Harvard University Press: Cambridge.

Tabb, J. Y., and Godfarb (Galin), A. (1970). *Workers' Participation in Management: Expectations and Experience*. Pergamon: Oxford.

Tang, T. L. P., and Butler, E. A. (1997). Attributions of Quality Circles' Problem-Solving Failure: Differences Among Management, Supporting Staff, and Quality Circle Members. *Public Personnel Management*. 26, 203–225.

Tannenbaum, A. S., and Kahn, R. L. (1958). *Participation in Union Locals*. Row Peterson: Evanston, IL.

Thompson, J. D. (1967). *Organizations in action*. McGraw-Hill: New York.

Trist, E. L., and Murray, H. (Eds.) (1993). *The Social Engagement of Social Science: A Tavistock Anthology: The Socio-technical Perspective*. Vol. II. University of Pennsylvania Press: Philadelphia.

Verma, A. (1989). Joint Participation Programs: Self-Help or Suicide for Labor? *Industrial Relations*. 28, 4, 401–411.

Verma, A., and McKersie, R. B. (1987). Employee Involvement: The Implications of Non-involvement by Unions. *Industrial and Labor Relations.* 40, 4, 556–568.

Wack, P. (1985). Scenarios: Uncharted Waters Ahead. *Harvard Business Review.* September-October, 72–89.

Wagner, J. A. (1994). Participation's Effects on Performance and Satisfaction: A Reconsideration of Research Evidence. *Academy of Management Review.* 19, 312–330.

Walker, K. (1976). Concepts of Industrial Democracy in International Perspective. In: Prichard, R. L. (Ed.). *Industrial Democracy in Australia.* CCH: Australia.

Walker, K. F. (1974). Workers' Participation in Management: Problems, Practice and Prospect. *International Institute of Labour Studies.* 12.

Wall, T. D., Kemp, N. J., Jackson, P. R., and Clegg, C. W. (1986). Outcomes of Autonomous Workgroups: A Long-Term Field Experiment. *Academy of Management Journal.* 29, 280–304.

Walton, R. (1975). Criteria for Quality of Working Life. In: Davis, L. E., and Cherns, A. B. (Eds.). *The Quality of Working Life.* The Free Press: New York.

Walton, R. E. (1982). Social Choice in the Development of Advanced Information Technology. *Human Relations.* 35, 12, 1037–1089.

Warner, M. (1984). *Organizations and Experiments: Designing New Ways of Managing Work.* Wiley: Chichester.

Webb, S., and Webb, B. (1902). *Industrial Democracy.* Longmans: London.

Weitzman, M. L., and Kruse, D. L. (1990). Profit Sharing and Productivity. In: Blinder, A. S. *Paying for Productivity: A Look at the Evidence.* Center for Economic Progress and Employment series. Brookings Institution: Washington, DC.

Westley, W. A. (1972). An Evaluation Model for Workers' Participation in management. *First International Conference on Participation and Self-Management.* Dubrovnik, 13–17 December, Vol. 2, 199–210.

Wilensky, H. L. (1956). Intellectuals in Labor Unions: Organizational Pressures on Professional Roles. The Free Press: Glencoe, IL.

Wilpert, B. (1975). Research on Industrial Democracy: The German Case. *Industrial Relations Journal.* 6, 53–64.

Withey, M. J., and Cooper, W H. (1989). Predicting Exit, Voice, Loyalty, and Neglect. *Administrative Science Quarterly.* 34, 521–539.

Witt, L. A. (1992). Exchange Ideology as a Moderator of the Relationships Between Importance of Participation in Decision-Making and Job Attitudes. *Human Relations.* 45, 1, 73–85.

Womack, J. P., Jones, D. T., and Roos, D. (1990). *The Machine that Changed the World*. Macmillan: New York.

Wood, S., and de Menezes, L. (1998). High Commitment Management in the UK: Evidence from the Workplace Industrial Relations Survey, and Employers' Manpower and Skills Practices Survey. *Human Relations*. 51, 4, 485–515

Wren, D. A. (1972). *The Evolution of Management Thought*. Ronald Press: New York.

Index

ABOUT THE AUTHOR

AVIAD BAR-HAIM heads the management and economics department at the Open University of Israel, Tel Aviv. He holds a doctorate in industrial sociology and organizational behavior from the Hebrew University of Jerusalem, and before his present assignment was the Open University's Dean for Academic Development. Among his current research and teaching interests are topics in organizational behavior and human resource management.